Homemade

with love ♡

Giving of oneself and one's time feels good, and
in a world often said to be divided between those
who spend money in order to save time and those
who spend time in order to save money,
our time is still seen as the ultimate luxury...

Homemade

Gorgeous things to make with love

Ros Badger and Elspeth Thompson

Photographs by Benjamin J Murphy

Collins

Dedication

To our mothers, Ruth and Margaret,
and our daughters, Martha, Ceidra and Mary,
who taught and continue to teach us so much

First published in 2009 by
Collins, an imprint of
HarperCollins Publishers
77–85 Fulham Palace Road
Hammersmith
London W6 8JB
www.collins.co.uk

Collins is a registered
trademark of HarperCollins
Publishers Ltd

10 9 8 7 6 5 4 3 2 1

Text © Ros Badger and
Elspeth Thompson 2009
Photography © Benjamin J
Murphy 2009

A catalogue record for this book
is available from the British
Library.

ISBN 978-0-00-728479-5

Photography Benjamin J Murphy
Editor Emma Callery
Design Andrew Barron
Illustrations Mary Mathieson,
Rosie Scott

Printed and bound by Leo Paper
Products Ltd.

Contents

Introduction

HOMEMADE. When searching for a title for this book, there was really only one candidate in our minds: this well-worn word that conjures up both things handmade at home, and a home that's made with love.

Home, for us, is where our creativity was nurtured and continues to grow. We were both born into families who, out of necessity as much as inclination, made clothes, grew their own vegetables and cooked from scratch rather than buying ready-made items from the shops. Ros can remember being taught to crochet, aged seven, by her grandmother, and making a doll's blanket of which she was inordinately proud. Elspeth only has to look at photographs of herself and her younger sisters in matching homemade dresses to be transported back to a happy, yet industrious, childhood where everyone seemed forever to be sewing, knitting or making things.

There was a time, not so very long ago, when 'homemade' had become synonymous with dowdiness, a degree of drudgery and doing without. From the profligate Eighties on, shopping was the preferred national pastime, while making your own was seen as second best, if not an eccentricity, or a leftover from childhood television programmes, such as *Blue Peter*.

Not so nowadays. Making things – whether sewing, cooking, or customizing clothes – is firmly in fashion, with clothes designers incorporating crochet and patchwork into their collections and celebrities as keen to be photographed with their knitting as they were with a yoga mat a few years ago. Wearing homemade clothes is something to be proud rather than ashamed of – living proof of your creativity and resourcefulness, as is sending homemade cards, or taking homemade jam, sweets or chutney as a dinner party gift. Making your own clothes or home furnishings is also a sure-fire way to get noticed in what is becoming an increasingly homogeneous society.

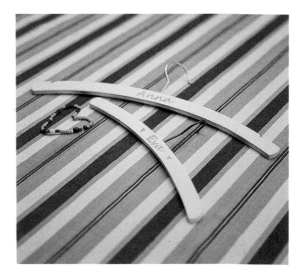

Of course, *Homemade* is not merely about style. What began as a gradual *zeitgeist* shift a few years ago – with a knitting and crochet revival, the resurgence in home-baking and general domesticity and everyone from New York bankers to teenage schoolgirls starting crafts clubs – has gained momentum recently, aided and abetted by the environmental and financial crises that face us all.

Making and growing things not only helps save money and is good for the environment (less manufacturing means less 'embodied energy' means less waste), the activities themselves give rise to a feel-good factor that can help cheer us up in adversity. Our homes become havens in times of global uncertainty, and knowing that we have the skills and resources to make things of use and beauty for those we live around and love – without costing the earth – can be a source of great comfort and pleasure. Making something for someone else with love, whether a cake for their birthday, a pair of warm woolly gloves or a simple greetings card, can be a satisfying thing to do in itself, for children and adults alike. Giving of oneself and one's time feels good, and in a world often said to be divided between those who spend money in order to spend time and those who save time in order to save money, our time is still seen as the ultimate luxury.

The 'homemade movement' is gathering momentum, with all sorts of people who may never have thought of making things becoming converts. This book is for them as much as for the more experienced, with many of the projects requiring no previous skills – and plenty of information on how to get started with knitting, crocheting, sewing and so on. How it differs from many of the other books and articles on similar subjects is that the sentiment expressed in the subtitle is more than skin deep. Many of the projects published elsewhere begin with a 'shopping list' of stuff to buy; surely something of a contradiction in terms if the aim is to be resourceful and economical.

What we'd far rather start off with is a new mindset – one that involves looking around and seeing what you have to start with, before going out to the shops. Saving fabric from favourite old clothes or furnishings, buttons from worn-out clothing and ribbon from unwrapped presents becomes second nature once you start – and as these saved and salvaged materials become stitched and woven into new objects, the backdrop to our lives gathers texture and richness, with added layers of memory and association. (We haven't quite reached the level of the old lady who claimed to have a tin in her attic labelled 'pieces of string too small to be useful', but sometimes we feel we are getting there!)

You will find that you start seeing potential in everything around you. Nature remains one of our greatest resources and, for this reason, the projects in the book are arranged around the seasons. As the saying goes, if life offers you lemons, make lemonade – and the changing months offer both new materials to use and colours and textures to be inspired by, as illustrated in the photographs of nature that appear throughout the book.

We hope that this approach will encourage you to try a few of the projects listed, maybe even adding to or adapting them according to your own ideas, inclinations and aspirations. Whatever you make, we hope you enjoy the process – and the feeling of pride and satisfaction that are part and parcel of the result. Most of all, we hope you will be able to take pleasure in saying, when asked where you bought or found the cake, dress or cushion in question: 'It's homemade. I made it myself.'

We haven't quite reached the level of the old lady who claimed to have a tin in her attic labelled 'pieces of string too small to be useful', but sometimes we feel we are getting there!

spring

Valentine's Day
ideas

SIDESTEP THE CRASS COMMERCIALIZATION of Valentine's Day with simple handmade gifts or tokens that mean so much more than shop-bought flowers or cards. The ideas shown on these pages are not at all difficult to make – indeed, some take only minutes – but are still lovely objects to treasure and keep. Paint a poem on to paper, customize vintage cards or make a paper cut-out by folding the paper concertina-style, marking a design in pencil and snipping out with sharp scissors. Write a message on a heart-shaped pebble, fashion a twiggy heart from whippy branches or thread beads or buttons on to fuse wire and bend into shape. Sometimes the simplest ideas are the most effective – surprise your partner with a heart formed from the family's shoes on the floor to greet them when they come downstairs in the morning, or write a quirky message in pebbles or leaves on the lawn.

♥ Thread buttons on to thick fuse wire, bend into shape and secure with a knot behind one of the buttons – pretty beads or sequins would work just as well.

Paint or chalk a message on a heart-shaped pebble – finding the pebble is the hard bit!

♥ Stitch together some scraps of fabric with romantic associations – from some favourite old shirts, for instance – and cut out two heart shapes. With right sides facing, sew together, leaving a small gap for turning through. Turn right sides out and use fancy traditional stitches to decorate the seams. Then stuff with dried lavender (see page 62) and stitch the gap to close.

Using pinking shears, cut out two heart shapes from contrasting colours of felt, one piece slightly smaller than the other. Embroider a simple message on the smaller one, and perhaps a few flowers, and attach to the other by sewing neatly around the edges. Add stick-on beads or sequins (if not using flowers) and a ribbon loop for hanging.

Egg
cosies

THESE COLOURFUL EGG COSIES, here and overleaf, will always cheer up your breakfast table as well as keeping your boiled eggs warm. Simple enough for quite small children to make under adult supervision, they also make great Easter presents, maybe decorated with the recipient's name and sitting on a nest of chocolate or marzipan eggs. Small items such as this are good ways of using up odd pieces of felt and thread, which might otherwise be wasted. And yet an egg cosy can definitely be defined as a luxury: a non-essential item that nevertheless enhances the enjoyment of one of life's simple pleasures.

You will need

◆ Pieces of felt and leftover scraps in different colours
◆ Sewing thread in various colours to contrast with the felt

To make the chicken cosy (opposite)

♥ Using the chicken pattern on page 236, cut out two pieces for the body and, in a contrasting colour, two pieces for the wings. Pin a wing to each chicken shape and sew the rounded end of the wings to the chicken's body using over stitch (see page 226).

♥ Make the eyes by stitching a star shape on each chicken piece in the middle of the head. Alternatively, sew a button on either side.

♥ Place the chicken pieces wrong sides together and pin to hold. Then sew around the chickens from the bottom right-hand corner to the bottom left-hand corner with blanket stitch, or running stitch if preferred (see pages 225–6). In a different colour, work blanket stitch along the bottom edge.

To make the simple cosy (page 23)

♥ Using the simple egg cosy pattern on page 236, cut out three pieces of felt in contrasting colours.

♥ Using scrap pieces of felt, decorate each piece with a motif of your choice. We cut out a flower for one of the cosies (you might choose to use the pattern on page 236) and letters for another (for example, 'EGG', 'DAD', 'MUM'). Sew on the motifs on with running stitch.

♥ Pin together two pieces of the cosy with wrong sides facing and sew along the seam with over stitch in a contrasting colour of thread. Add the third piece and sew along the two remaining seams with over stitch.

These colourful egg cosies will always cheer up your breakfast table.

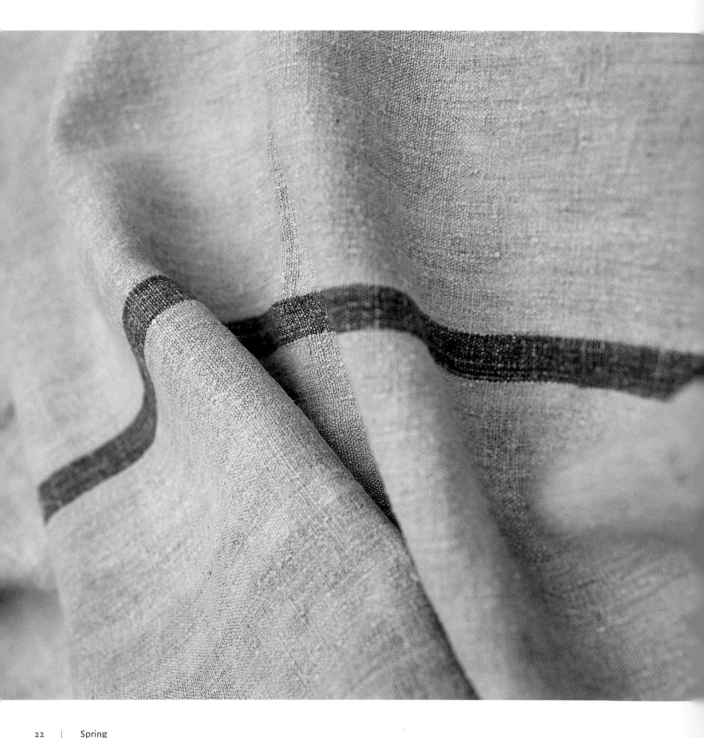

Pin the egg on the
chicken

THIS DELIGHTFUL PAINTED BANNER can be brought out every year for Easter parties or spring birthdays. Not only does it look decorative, it also provides the basis for good old-fashioned fun in the form of the traditional blindfold game – a variation on Pin the Tail on the Donkey.

You will need

- A plain cotton or linen sheet
- Washable paints or inks
- Assortment of paintbrushes
- Stiff paper or card
- Sticky tape
- A blindfold

To make and play

♥ Using the sheet as the canvas, apply your design with the washable paints or inks. See the tips on page 28 for copying and transferring pictures or designs on to fabric, or ask a talented friend or child to draw the pictures by hand.

♥ While the banner is drying, draw ten or so egg shapes on to the paper or card, decorate in an assortment of egg colours and cut out when dry. Just before you play the game, add a loop of sticky tape to the back of each egg for attaching it to the banner. This is much safer for children than using pins.

♥ To play the game, hang the banner against a wall or from the branches of a low-growing tree – we pegged ours to a washing line (see overleaf). Blindfold each player by turn, spin them around slowly twice, pencil their name on the back of an egg and ask them to attach it to the picture as near to where the chicken would have laid it as they can. When everyone has had a go, the winner is the one whose egg is nearest to the right place.

Variations

Make a series of seasonal banners for party fun throughout the year: pin the nose (or broom) on the witch for Hallowe'en; the horns on the reindeer for Christmas; the wand on the fairy or the cherry on the cake for all-purpose birthdays, and so on. The possibilities are endless!

Tips on handpainting

Several of the projects in this book were handpainted by Mary Mathieson (as well as the Easter banner on the previous page, see also the Lavender cats on page 62 and the Advent calendar on page 202). If you are not particularly artistic yourself, it may be worth commissioning a clever friend or acquaintance to help with some of the ideas, particularly if, like the banner and calendar, they have the potential to become family heirlooms. But it is important not to be too precious about these things. Children's drawings have a wonderful spontaneity about them, which it would be fun to preserve. Simple potato prints and/or abstract freehand patterns can look great if you choose the right colours. And your own freehand attempts may surprise you, if you are bold enough to try.

♥ Try copying an existing design, using graph paper and tracing paper. The internet is a fabulous instant source of all kinds of patterns and images that can be copied or customized. Just click on to Google Images and search for the type of picture or pattern you want. You can also search for fonts for letters, as used for the Painted hangers on page 41. Print out the design, scale it up using graph paper (if necessary) and then transpose, using tracing paper and pencil, to the place where it is needed.

♥ Use fabric paints or fabric crayons to colour in and define your design. These come in many colours, including metallic shades. Don't be afraid to make sweeping strokes and be creative – freehand drawing buzzes with creative energy.

♥ Before making your decorated fabric into banners, clothes or soft furnishings, fix the fabric paint or crayon designs in place by ironing them as the instructions specify. Your design should then be machine washable.

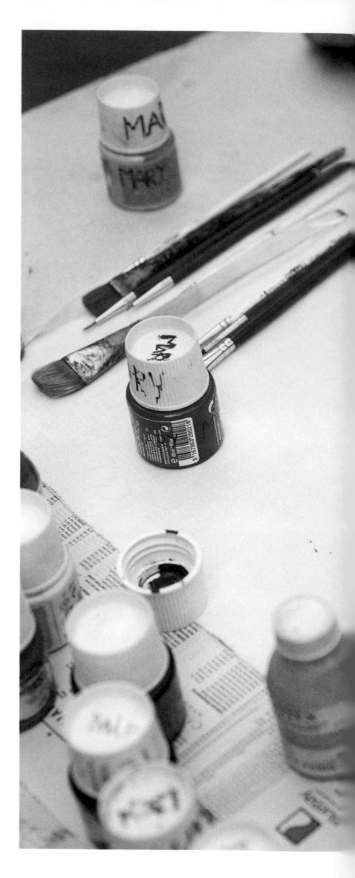

Natural
cleaning materials

ONCE YOU'VE GOT into the *Homemade* mindset, you may find that mixing your own cleaning materials from natural ingredients makes more sense than using specific cleaning products. Why spend money filling your cupboards with garishly packaged potions and powders, often brimming with chemicals that can cause allergies and other health problems, when these natural, cheap and readily available solutions work just as well, if not better – and often smell sweeter, to boot? Here are just a few we have found effective.

DRAINS: Once a month, pour a kettle full of boiling water over a cup or two of soda crystals in order to keep your drains free and fragrant.

FINGER MARKS ON WALLS AND PAINTWORK: Rub with a chunk of fresh white bread.

GROUTING ON TILES: Scrub with a toothbrush, using a paste made from bicarbonate of soda and lemon juice.

LIMESCALE IN KETTLES: Fill with distilled white vinegar and leave overnight. Rinse well afterwards.

LIMESCALE ON TAPS: Rub with a paste of distilled white vinegar and bicarbonate of soda. Or soak a paper towel in fresh lemon juice, wrap around the tap, cover with a plastic bag and leave overnight. Wipe clean.

MILDEW: Wipe with distilled white vinegar.

POTS AND PANS: Add to half a cup of soap flakes mixed with enough water to fill the pan. When cold, wash up.

REFRIGERATOR: Wipe all the surfaces inside with a paste of one tablespoon of bicarbonate of soda in a little hot water (also dispels odours).

SMELLY PET BEDDING OR ODOROUS TRAINERS: Sprinkle with bicarbonate of soda overnight and shake or brush out the next day.

STAINED TEA AND COFFEE CUPS: Brush with a paste of bicarbonate of soda and a little water.

STUBBORN STAINS ON BATHS AND/OR BASINS: Wipe with a paste of bicarbonate of soda and water or cream of tartar and lemon juice.

TILED FLOORS: Wash with a mix made from equal quantities of water and distilled white vinegar.

UNIVERSAL FABRIC STAIN REMOVER: Dab the stained fabric with fresh lemon juice and leave in strong sunlight, or (for more sensitive colours and fabrics) rub with soda crystals before hand washing.

WINDOWS: Wipe with distilled white vinegar and rub dry with newspaper. For very dirty panes, sponge with eco-friendly washing-up liquid first.

Easter
tree

HANGING HAND-DECORATED EGGS on branches of spring leaves and blossom is
a lovely tradition that can become part of family life. Those in the picture are a
mixture of hand-painted and decorated eggshells, some of which date back
20 years or more, treasures given by friends or family or brought back from
trips abroad. If you make and buy a few more eggs each year, you will soon
have an heirloom collection that can be handed down to the next generation.

You will need

- Raw eggs
- Empty egg box
- Darning needle
- Bowl
- Vinegar
- Paints, felt pens, pastels, glue, paper and fabric scraps –
  whatever comes to hand for decorating
- Food colouring and/or onion skins (optional)
- Ribbon or fine cord with beads
- Small branches for the 'tree'

To make

♥ To blow a raw egg, place it upright in the egg box and use
a darning needle to make a small hole in the top. Turn the
egg carefully upside down and make a slightly larger hole in
the bottom. Break up the yolk by poking the needle about
inside, and then gently, but steadily, blow into the smaller
hole to evacuate the innards into a bowl (save for making
scrambled eggs or pancakes).

♥ Rinse the egg by by submerging the shell in water with a
little vinegar added and blowing out again. Allow to dry.

♥ Decorating ideas include painting with poster paints, felt
pens or pastels – anything from free-form flowers, chicks and
rabbits to polka dots, stripes, spirals or designs that run
around the circumference of the shell. Or stick on paper,
fabric, pressed or imitation flowers or other shapes – adding
ribbons, bows or other ornamentation as the fancy takes you.

♥ Most eggs have brown shells these days, but how about
using blue for a change? Or, to dye white eggshells, add a few
drops of food colouring (or create a natural dye such as from
onion skins for a rich ochre yellow) to a pan of water with the
eggshells and simmer for 10 minutes.

♥ To attach the eggs to the tree, cut a length of ribbon and
glue it carefully right around the egg lengthwise, tying the
free ends into a bow at the top. Alternatively, thread one end
of a fine cord or ribbon through the darning needle and tie a
knot in the other end. Thread a small bead on to the cord or
ribbon and pass the needle through the large hole at the base
of the egg and out through the smaller hole at the top. The
bead should then anchor the cord or ribbon in place,
allowing you to make a loop for tying at the top of the egg.

♥ After Easter, store the eggs in the empty egg box in a safe
place until next year.

...a lovely tradition that can become part of family life...

Decorated
coat hangers

DECORATED COAT HANGERS not only look good in your wardrobe, but they are practical, too, as the texture of the knitted and crocheted covers stop silky clothes from slipping off. They also make a lovely present, particularly if they are personalized with the recipient's name or some other detail. A hand-covered or painted hanger can also add that extra, personal touch when giving home-sewn, hand-me-down or vintage clothes. You might be forgiven for thinking that the examples pictured here are time-consuming to make, but they are surprisingly quick and easy. The hanger used is a standard wooden one, 45cm (18in) long and 2cm (¾in) wide – but you could make a shorter cover to fit a standard child's hanger, which is 32cm (12½in) long.

Knitted cover with optional crochet flower

The knitted cover pictured opposite is so simple that anyone able to cast on and off and do basic garter stitch could make it. There is no purl stitch, no shaping – just a simple strip like a doll's scarf. It is a great way to use up odd scraps of wool – the method below specifies 4-ply, but any weight of wool will do. Cast on stitches the width of the hanger front and back, and knit in garter stitch until the length of the hanger has been reached.

You will need

◆ 1 x 50g (2oz) ball 4-ply mercerized cotton (or matt cotton) for main colour (MC)
◆ Ends of 4-ply mercerized cotton (or matt cotton) in contrast colour for crotchet flower (optional)
◆ 2.75mm (UK size 12; US size 2) knitting needles
◆ 2mm crochet hook
◆ Wooden coat hanger
◆ Darning needle
◆ PVA glue (optional)

Tension over garter stitch

26sts and 48 rows = 10cm (4in)

Abbreviations

See pages 229 and 231

Measurements

45cm (18in) on top curve of coat hanger

To make the hanger cover

♥ With 2.75mm (UK size 12; US size 2) needles and MC, cast on 17sts.
Work in garter st (knit every row) until strip measures length of coat hanger when slightly stretched.
Cast off.
Find the centre of work in both length and width and slip over hanger hook.
Stitch the strip together on the underside of the hanger with a neat catch st. Sew both ends to close.

To cover a standard (13.5cm/5¼in) hook (optional)

♥ With 2.75mm (UK size 12; US size 2) needles and MC, cast on 38sts (measure your hanger hook and adjust accordingly). Work 4 rows in garter st.

Cast off.

Fold around hook and sew edges together so the hook is covered.

Catch to hanger cover to avoid hook cover slipping off. Alternatively, wrap the hook with the yarn, securing at each end with a blob of PVA glue.

To make the crochet flower (optional)

♥ With 2mm crochet hook and contrast colour, make 6ch and join with a sl st.

Row 1: Work 15dc into the circle, join with a sl st.
Row 2: 1ch, 1dc in first dc,* 3ch, 1dc into 3rd dc, repeat from *. End with 3ch then sl st to 1st dc.

Row 3: 1ch, work a petal of (1dc, 3ch, 5tr, 3ch, 1dc) into each of next 5 3ch arches, sl st to 1st dc.
Row 4: 1ch, (1dc between 2dc, 5ch behind petal of 3rd round) 5 times, sl st to first dc.
Row 5: 1ch, work a petal of (1dc, 3ch, 7tr, 3ch, 1dc) into each of the 5 5ch arches, sl st to 1st dc.
Sew flower to centre of hanger.

Crocheted cover

If you are able to crochet, this cover is very pretty, using two colours of yarn in a textured pattern. If making it to go with a gift of clothes, choose colours to coordinate with them. Treasured clothes from your children's early childhood can also be hung on these hangers from the walls of their bedrooms (like the Child's summer dresses on page 72).

You will need

◆ 2 x 25g (1oz) 4-ply cotton or wool in contrasting colours
◆ 2.25mm crochet hook
◆ Wooden coat hanger
◆ PVA glue

Abbreviations

See page 231

Measurements

45cm (18in) on top curve of coat hanger or 32cm (12½in) child's coat hanger

To make 2

♥ The shell pattern is made up of a multiple of 6ch plus 3 turning chain. So reduce or add by 6, depending on the length of your coat hanger.

This pattern is worked as 4 rows either side of the central 100(76) chain with rows 5 and 6 worked all around the work.

♥ With 2.25mm crochet hook and 4-ply yarn, make 100(76)ch.

Row 1: Work 2tr in 4th chain from hook, * miss 2ch, 1dc in next ch, miss 2ch, 5tr in next ch. Repeat from * to end, finishing with 1dc in last chain.

Row 2: NB this row is worked along the base of chain. Sl st into side of lst dc from row 1, then work 3ch, 2tr into first ch (where last dc from row 1 was made), * miss 2ch, 1dc (into chain where last group of 5tr were made on the previous row), miss 2ch, 5tr into next ch. Repeat from * to end, finishing with 1 dc at end.

Row 3: Change colour, 3ch, 2tr on top of last dc from row 2, * 1dc either side of the centre treble of the 5tr cluster from row 2, 3tr in next dc. Repeat from * to end.

Row 4: Sl st down side of work and repeat row 3 above row 1.

Rows 5 & 6: Dc all around the edge of work. Fasten off.

To JOIN: Place two pieces together, wrong sides facing. Sl st together along bottom edge and half of top. Then place on to hanger and finish sl stitching together on to the hanger. Leave the hook bare or bind it using a length of the yarn, securing at each end with a blob of PVA glue.

Painted hangers

For tips on choosing typefaces and tracing and transferring images from your computer, see page 28.

♥ To ensure a good finish, use a couple of coats of gloss paint in your chosen colour, and allow to dry completely before adding your design or name in a contrasting colour.

♥ Use as little paint as is needed to create an even coverage and flat finish. It will also keep drips to a minimum. When applying the background colour, paint the entire hanger and hang it on a clothesline (or similar) to dry, with newspaper beneath to catch any drips.

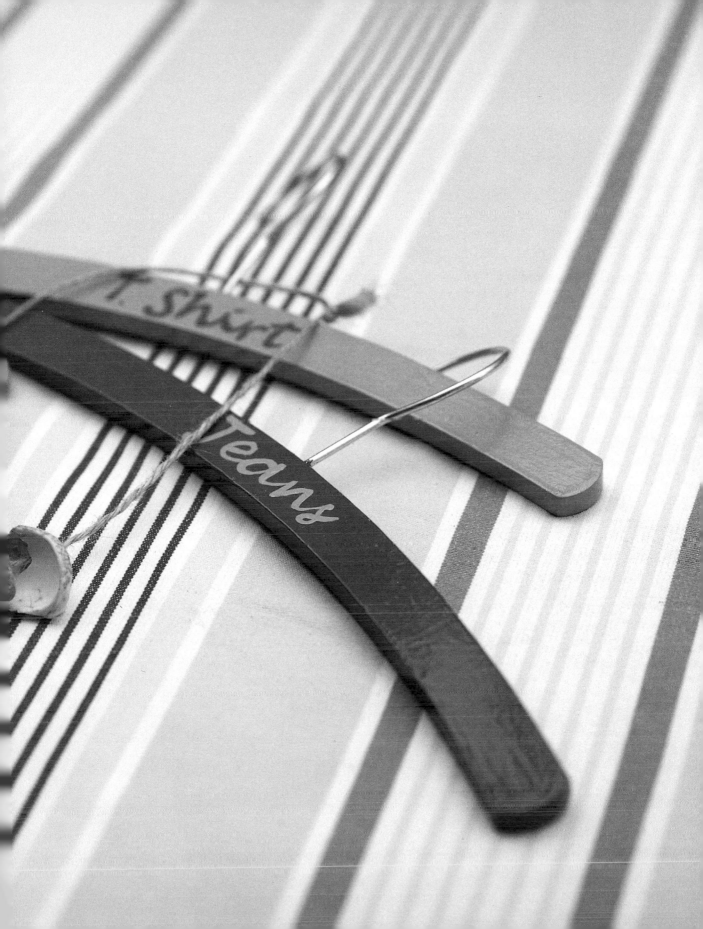

Patchwork wall

WE LOVE PATCHWORK, both for its simple graphic patterns and the mêlée of memories and associations it can evoke. Projects such as covering a wall with scraps of paper, as here, give patchwork a modern spin, while losing none of its timeless charm and appeal. Choose just one wall in a room – alcoves or chimneybreasts work well – or it will look overwhelming, though you might get away with it in a small downstairs loo. Gather lots of scraps of wallpaper. Old sample books are a great source if you can get hold of any from wallpaper shops or suppliers, otherwise raid your attic and homes of friends for leftover rolls to cut up. Like traditional fabric patchwork, this idea has far more resonance if patterns with sentimental value – the paper from your childhood bedroom or first married home, for example – are included in the mix.

You will need

- Wallpaper scraps or samples
- Plumb line
- Spirit level
- Wallpaper paste and brush
- Water and sponge
- Stepladder

To make

♥ Decide on a rough colour scheme and plan how you will cover the space, distributing strong colours, patterns and different sizes throughout. How precisely you work is a matter of personal style and temperament – perfectionists will do a trial run with Blu-tac and use a plumb line to ensure all the verticals are straight, while others will be happy to stick as they go.

♥ Paste small patches of pattern at a time, butting the edges neatly against one another and cutting pieces to fit wherever necessary. Keep checking progress by standing well back to assess the effect, and when finished, sit back or lie down and drift into each pattern in turn.

Variations

Other possibilities for this treatment include postcards, cartoons, book jackets (an example of this seen in a bookshop in New York), sheet music or maps.

Sowing
seeds

RAISING PLANTS FROM SEED is a satisfying pastime – and it saves money, too. A packet of lettuce or rocket seeds doesn't cost very much and, if sown in small batches at fortnightly intervals, will keep you in salad leaves all summer – just look at the price of lettuce in supermarkets and you will see what a saving this is. Your own produce can also be grown organically, without the use of artificial feeds or pesticides, and harvested at the peak of freshness. Ornamental plants for the garden border or containers can also be started off in this way – choose annuals like sunflowers and cosmos, which germinate fast and don't need the extra heat of a greenhouse.

Starting seeds off in pots or trays is often useful, as it means the seedlings are easily identified from the 'weedlings' that might spring up in open ground, and the young plants can be protected from slugs and snails until they are larger and stronger. Smaller seeds, for such plants as lettuce or violas, are best sown in trays and transplanted, or 'pricked out', into pots when the first 'true' leaves have formed, handling gently by the first leaves, not the delicate stems.

Avoid using plastic pots and trays, which cost energy to produce, are non-biodegradable and only just becoming recyclable. Instead, try to use longer-lasting wooden trays, such as those pictured overleaf (which can be personally printed), and for pots, look for salvaged terracotta, biodegradable coir or DIY versions made from newspapers (see page 48). Always label your sowings. Recycled lolly sticks or wooden stirrers for hot drinks are attractive and reusable.

You will need

- ◆ Seed tray(s) or 7.5cm (3in) pots
- ◆ Seed compost
- ◆ Sheet of glass or plastic, or small plastic bags (for pots)
- ◆ Newspaper
- ◆ Trowel

To sow in trays

♥ Fill the tray to the top with seed compost (ordinary compost is too rich in nutrients), level off and soak with water using a watering can with a medium rose head. Sprinkle the seed sparingly over the surface of the soil and cover with a fine layer of compost.

♥ Place a sheet of glass (or a plastic cover) and newspaper on top and do not water again. Check every 24 hours – some seeds germinate in a matter of days – and remove the glass and newspaper when the seedlings are up. Prick out the healthiest plants into small pots when the second set of leaves have formed.

To sow in pots

♥ Larger seeds, such as sunflowers, courgettes or broad beans, can be sown two or three to a 7.5cm (3in) pot. Fill the pots with seed compost to the top and water well. Then, push one seed at a time down into the soil at the recommended depth and cover with soil.

♥ Cover with glass, or a plastic bag secured with an elastic band, to speed up germination. If the seeds all germinate, select the strongest one or two for planting out.

♥ Once the seedlings are established, keep well watered using a watering can with a fine rose head. Plant out in open ground when the roots are just beginning to emerge through the drainage holes and any danger of frost has passed.

Planting out into soil or large containers

♥ Well before your seedlings are large enough to be planted out, clear the ground they are to go into of weeds, giving it one last hoe or weed before the young plants go in. If the soil needs improving, work in some well-rotted compost or manure, or fork in a handful of organic fertilizer, such as seaweed or blood, fish and bone, per square metre.

♥ To plant, dig a hole at least three times the size of the rootball and water it well. Knock the plant gently out of its pot and place in the hole, filling loosely with compost and soil, so the soil levels for the plant and ground are equal. You can plant newspaper (see overleaf) and coir pots straight in the ground. Keep the plants well watered in hot, dry spells.

♥ If growing vegetables, harvest for cooking as required, trimming the plant regularly and removing at least some of the flowers to ensure plenty of fresh new growth. Remember, too, that you can collect your own seed for sowing next year.

Newspaper pots

You can buy kits to make newspaper pots – those that make more than one at a time are obviously less laborious. They all entail tearing old newspapers into strips and coiling them up to make containers to fill with compost for sowing.

The individual wooden 'pot makers' can easily be emulated by using a length of broomstick, wrapping a double thickness of newspaper about 20cm (8in) long around it and over the rounded end and slipping carefully off, scrunching up one end for the base of the pot. Placing the paper pots in old egg boxes helps keep them from unravelling or falling apart when watered. The joy is that the pots can be planted straight into open ground, when the time comes, without disturbing the plants' roots.

Recycled lolly sticks make attractive, reusable labels.

Easter trug

FLORISTS' SHOPS and garden centres are full of pretty spring bulbs in pots at this time of year, so pick your favourites and make an impromptu Easter garden in a traditional trug or basket. This would make a great centrepiece for the Easter lunch table, or could be given as a present. For a lovely naturalistic look, we chose plants that might be found in a country hedgerow – primroses, snakeshead fritillaries (*Fritillaria meleagris*) and dwarf daffodils (2–3 of each for a medium trug, with self-seeding purple-leafed violets dug up from the garden as an edging). Once the flowers are over, the plants can be set out in the garden (or in a large pot) for next year, and the trug or basket pressed into use.

You will need

- A traditional wooden trug or basket
- Outdoor eggshell paint (see Directory, page 242)
- Paintbrush
- Black bin liner or compost bag
- General-purpose potting compost
- Assortment of potted spring-flowering bulbs or other flowers in bud

To make

♥ If using a trug, give it a couple of coats of eggshell paint and leave to dry.

♥ Line the inside of the trug or basket with plastic, cutting so that it comes just below the rim. Use a knife to make two or three slits in the base of the plastic for drainage, and anchor it in position with a handful of compost.

♥ Experiment with positioning your plants (still in pots) inside the trug until you have an attractive arrangement – tallest plants in the centre, descending in height to groundcover varieties around the edges usually works best.

♥ Knock the plants gently out of their pots. Depending on the height of the soil in the pots, either add a layer of compost to the base of the trug first, or start positioning your plants, working from the centre outwards.

♥ Fill in any gaps between the plants with extra compost, or with smaller plug plants or little violet or viola seedlings.

♥ Press down gently around the plants with your fingers and water well. Keep the compost moist but not sodden while the plants are in flower – they will dry out more quickly if they are kept indoors.

Thyme
carpet in a crate

Buzzing with bees and studded with fragrant flowers in summer, a carpet of different thyme plants is a lovely idea. If you don't have room in your garden to plant one, don't despair! This potted version uses an old wooden box or crate instead of a sunny bank – a shallow basket would work equally well as thyme is shallow-rooted, needing only 10cm (4in) or so of soil. Choose a variety of different types of thyme with contrasting leaf sizes, scents and colours for an attractive – and aromatic – effect. There are lemon-scented and gold- and silver-leaved species, as well as the more common broad-leaved and small-leaved types (see Directory, pages 247–9). Harvest the leaves to bring flavour to salads and cooked dishes.

You will need
- Various thyme plants to cover surface of soil
- Wooden crate, box or basket
- Black bin liner or compost bag
- Gravel, bricks or polystyrene chips
- All-purpose compost

To make
♥ Water your plants well before planting. Place them in their pots in a large pot or tray of water for a good soaking while you prepare the container.

♥ Line the inside of the box or basket with plastic, cutting so that it comes just below the rim. Use a knife to make two or three slits in the base of the plastic for drainage. Place gravel, bricks or polystyrene chips in the base of the container to improve the drainage and save on compost, leaving space for 10–15cm (4–6in) of compost at the top.

♥ Add enough compost so that the soil in the pots is level with the top of the container (it will settle to a lower level later). Plan your arrangement with the plants still in their pots, then knock them gently out, tease out the roots a little and plant in position. Fill in with compost between the plants and water thoroughly.

♥ Place in a sunny spot and keep well watered for the first few weeks. Harvest for cooking as required.

Harvest the leaves to bring flavour to salads and cooked dishes...

Elderflower
cordial

WITH ITS FRESH, flowery taste and fragrant aroma, elderflower cordial seems to distil the very essence of spring and early summer into a bottle. It is also incredibly easy to make. For the best flavour, gather your flowers on a warm sunny morning, and pick only those whose flowerheads are fully open and still dusty with floury yellowish pollen. Decanted into pretty bottles, with handwritten labels, this would make the perfect gift for bringing to a dinner party or weekend away. It is also lovely as a base for champagne cocktails, a sauce over ice cream, or added to a gooseberry fool to enhance its flavour. It keeps in the fridge for several weeks – if you can resist it for that long – or can be frozen in plastic bags or bottles. Some recipes require boiling but this one doesn't and so retains the true flavour of the elderflowers.

You will need

- 10 large heads of elderflowers (see above for when to pick them)
- 900ml (1½ pints) boiling water
- 680g (1½lb) unrefined caster sugar or a mixture of caster sugar and muscovado
- 3–4 lemons, strips of zest removed and the fruit sliced
- Sterlized bottles (see page 233)

To make

♥ Place the elderflowers in a large stainless steel pan or plastic bucket, pour over the boiling water, add the sugar and stir. Add the lemon slices, squeezing as you do so to release their juice, and stir in the zest.

♥ Cover with a clean damp cloth and leave somewhere cool and dark to steep for 48 hours. Strain through a sieve lined with muslin and decant into the sterilized bottles.

Variations

♥ Use 25g (1oz) of citric/tartaric acid instead of lemons. This may enhance the keeping potential of the cordial, although fresh lemons give the best flavour.

♥ If you are unable to find elderflowers, fruit cordials can be made by pouring 500ml (18fl oz) of boiling water over 450g (1lb) of fresh fruit, such as strawberries, raspberries or blackcurrants. Then add 900g (2lb) of caster sugar, one zested and sliced lemon and 40g (1½oz) of citric/tartaric acid. Cover and leave somewhere cool and dark for 48 hours before decanting as above.

Simnel cake

WITH THEIR 11 BALLS of marzipan representing the Apostles (minus Judas, who betrayed Jesus), simnel cakes are traditional Easter fare. This recipe is a lighter version of Christmas cake, with the marzipan incorporated into the cake as well as covering it in the traditional way. Leave plain for a wholesome, minimalist look, or add a central 'nest' made from cornflakes mixed with butter, cocoa and a little golden syrup, filled (and re-filled) with foil- or sugar-coated eggs.

You will need

- 225g (8oz) butter, softened
- 225g (8oz) soft brown sugar
- 3 eggs
- 3 tbsp milk
- 350g (12oz) self-raising flour, sifted
- 350g (12oz) mixed dried fruit
- 50g (2oz) mixed dried peel
- 110g (4oz) natural glacé cherries
- 1 tsp mixed spice
- 1 tbsp black treacle
- At least 350g (12oz) natural marzipan
- Apricot jam, for securing marzipan
- 1 egg, beaten, for glazing

To make

♥ Preheat the oven to 150°C (300°F), Gas 2. Grease and line a 20cm (8in) diameter spring-form cake tin with parchment paper.

♥ Put the butter and sugar in a bowl and, using a hand-held electric whisk, cream together until light and fluffy. Add the eggs and milk and continue to beat together. Add the remaining ingredients, except the marzipan, and stir well. Smooth half the mixture into the base of the cake tin.

♥ Divide the marzipan into three equal parts. Form one piece into a ball and roll out to make a 20cm (8in) round. Place on top of the mixture in the cake tin before adding the rest of the mixture.

♥ Bake on the bottom shelf of the oven for 1 hour. Then turn down the temperature to 140°C (275°F), Gas 1 and cook for a further hour or until the top is brown, firm and just springy to the touch. Take care not to overcook the cake – it is best if the middle is still a little soft and squidgy; test by inserting a skewer into the centre. Remove the cake from the oven and leave to cool.

♥ In a small bowl, dilute 3 tablespoons of the jam with 1 tablespoon of hot water. Roll out another marzipan disc to fit the top of the cake, and use a little diluted jam to secure it in place. Make 11 balls from the remaining marzipan and position at regular intervals (again secured with a little diluted jam) around the top of the cake.

♥ Preheat the grill to medium. Brush the marzipan lightly with egg and glaze under the grill for 1–2 minutes until slightly browned, taking care not to burn the marzipan. Wrap the cake in foil to store until needed (it will last for several weeks), and decorate further as you wish.

summer

Lavender cats

LAVENDER BAGS have a somewhat quaint, old-fashioned image, but there is no reason why they cannot be updated. These hand-painted lavender cats were made as presents for Ros's daughters by our friend the artist Mary Mathieson (see Directory, page 251). They can be made in any size – tiny ones for tucking into drawers to keep clothes fresh and protect against moths, or large enough to double up as fragrant cushions. Adding dried beans to the lavender mix for the larger cats not only makes it go further but adds some welcome weight to the cushions. They make wonderful presents – and can be personalized with a name.

You will need

◆ Dried lavender or lavender bush for drying at home
◆ Plain cotton fabric (an old sheet is fine)
◆ Fabric paints and crayons
◆ Paintbrushes
◆ Cotton thread for machine or hand sewing

To make

♥ If you have lavender in your garden, you can dry your own flowers. Harvesting just as the top florets are opening ensures the strongest scent, but after flowering, when the blooms are already drying on the stems, is also fine. Cut the flowers with long stems, tie with string in bunches of 30 or so stems. Place the head of each bunch in a brown paper bag, tie up with string and hang, flowers downwards, in a dry place for ten days to two weeks. When the flowers are fully dry, open the bags and pull off any remaining florets that have not fallen from the stems.

♥ To make the fabric cat bag, transfer the cat pattern on page 237 on to a piece of cotton fabric folded into two. Cut around the design, leaving 1cm (½in) all around as a seam allowance. Paint the pieces with fabric paints or crayons (see page 28 for handpainting tips). Iron to fix the design as on the following product instructions.

♥ Turn right sides together and machine or hand sew around the outline, leaving a gap of about 5cm (2in) along the bottom edge for stuffing. Snip in towards the seam on the curved edges so the bag lies flat when opened out.

♥ Turn right sides out and iron into shape, using the pointed ends of scissors to push out any awkward corners. Stuff with dried lavender – or lavender mixed with small dried beans (such as mung) – and neatly hand sew up the opening. Make sure not to get the lavender cat wet, especially if beans have been included.

Variations

If you don't feel confident about making a cat, why not make a simple square or heart shape and decorate with abstract patterns or even potato prints? Remember that you can decorate the back, too.

Modern patchwork

FOR CENTURIES, making patchwork has provided an attractive, economical and absorbing way to turn scraps of old fabric into objects of real beauty. Traditionally, patchworking was made in poorer areas, as witnessed by the 'kantha' cloths of India, hand-quilted from strips of old patterned saris; the patched 'Boro' overalls of Japanese cotton workers, in which the original garment is scarcely identifiable beneath the patches; and the traditional American quilts of the Midwest with their descriptive names – 'Log Cabin', 'Tumbling Dice' and 'Grandmother's Flower Garden'. Love, memories and companionship, as well as thrift, went into these pieces, which were often made in groups or quilting circles, and were handed down through generations of women. Ironically, with the passing of time, many of these once humble items are now hugely valuable, commanding high prices in antiques shops and auction rooms.

Patchwork is certainly fashionable again, with many people trying their hand at making their own, as well as collecting old examples. Some are drawn to the old patterns and techniques, using templates and intricate hand sewing. But patchwork can be given a modern spin, the homespun aesthetic partnered with sharp contemporary tailoring, as in designs by Paul Smith and Vivienne Westwood, or with sleek modern furniture, such as the silk patchwork cushions on classic white plastic Saarinen chairs, seen in the window of the Designer's Guild shop. We even spotted an amazing patchwork sofa by Squint (see Directory, page 251). (See also the Patchwork wall featured on page 42.)

Such ambitious projects may be somewhere down the line, unless you are already a patchwork aficionado, but there's no reason why patchwork has to be fussy and fiddly. Start saving pieces of fabric now – from favourite outgrown children's clothes, shirts that have worn at the collars and/or elbows, jeans too frayed and faded to wear. Put together in the right way, they too can become latter-day heirlooms every bit as valuable as those of the past – not least to your family, who will enjoy pointing out their old school prize day dresses, the birthday frock, the all-time-favourite shirt or pair of trousers. See the projects on the next pages for ideas for making patchwork designs that are simple, modern and stylish.

Patchwork
throw

Patchwork is as fiddly as you want to make it. Complex designs using cutout templates and tiny hand-sewn stitches are all very well, but few of us have the time these days. The modern 'cheat's' approach is to machine-sew together the fragments of fabric, first of all in strips, and then joining the strips of fabric together to form a flat piece of material that can then be cut to create clothing or used to upholster furniture. This eye-catching throw, inspired by a piece by stylist Kristin Perers (see Directory, page 251), uses strips of worn and faded denim, striped ticking and the edges of vintage linen tea towels. Far easier than re-upholstering a sofa, it's a great way to put to use the parts of pairs of jeans too worn to wear, or the unsullied borders of singed or stained tea towels, which can be picked up cheaply in second-hand shops.

You will need

◆ Assorted pieces of denim, ticking and tea towels
◆ Cotton thread for machine sewing
◆ Old sheet, blanket or length of fabric

To make

♥ Choose which pieces of fabric you are going to work with. You want a good distribution of colours, stripes and textures throughout – it will always show if you run out towards the end and have to start again with new material.

♥ Cut strips and squares of random length but more or less the same width – here they are 15–20cm (6–8in). On the throw in the photograph, the stripes face the same way on alternating strips, so if you want to do the same thing, divide your fabric into two equal piles and arrange them so that the stripes are vertical for one half and horizontal for the other.

♥ Machine them together in strips in a well-spaced yet random-looking order, with all the stripes facing the appropriate direction. Make enough strips to join together to form the throw.

♥ Pin or tack the strips together, with stripes facing upwards one row, crossways the next. Machine together.

♥ Trim the seams, trimming away large overlaps where necessary, and iron into shape.

♥ Make a backing using an old sheet or blanket or, if you have it, a large length of striped canvas or similar, of contrasting or coordinating colours. Cut this to the same size as the patchwork piece, place right sides together and machine around the edge, as if making a huge cushion, leaving a little gap along one edge. Turn right sides out through this gap, sew up and iron into shape. With any leftover fabric, make a couple of cushion covers to match.

This eye-catching throw uses strips of worn and faded denim, striped ticking and the edges of vintage linen tea towels.

Denim
chair

Old denim jeans are great for patchwork, as the flies, pockets and worn and faded patches all add interest. Cutting up a pair of jeans and sewing the bits together to make a flat piece of fabric can be the basic starting point for any number of projects, from cushion covers to simple upholstery. This director's chair was covered in this way, and is incredibly effective, looking much more complicated to make than, in fact, it is.

You will need

- A director's chair that has seen better days
- Sandpaper and wood treatment (optional)
- Pair of old denim jeans or denim off-cuts
- Cotton thread for machine sewing
- Hammer and nails or staple gun

To make

♥ Remove the sling seat and back from an old director's chair and keep as a pattern piece. If the wood is worn or stained, you can sand it down and, if necessary, re-varnish at this stage.

♥ Cut up the denim jeans or off-cuts into pieces that are a similar width but of varying lengths. Stitch together to make two flat pieces of fabric, each roughly the size of the seat and back pieces you have removed. Depending on the size and condition of the jeans, it may be possible to create quite large pieces (as in the photograph) with not too much sewing involved. Allow 2cm (¾in) extra at the top and bottom edges to hem and at least 8cm (3¼in) at the sides for attaching to the chair frame. The easiest way to stitch together the denim pieces is using a sewing machine to first make strips and then sew them together. Trim the seams to neaten.

♥ When deciding which piece of fabric is going where, keep in mind where interesting features on the jeans will appear on the finished chair – we used the fly detail for the back and a pair of pockets for the seat. Make sure the seat, in particular, is made from strong, unworn pieces, as it will be taking the most weight.

♥ Turn over the top and bottom edges of each patchworked piece and hem by hand or machine, using the original seat covers as a guide.

♥ Wrap the edges around the chair frame so that the raw edges are hidden, and then nail or staple the back and seat securely into place.

Child's
summer dress

We both grew up wearing pretty floral dresses like the one pictured opposite, and Elspeth's mother has continued the tradition by making two summer and two winter dresses from patterns such as this one for every year of her grand-daughter Mary's childhood. With simple classic childrenswear coming back into fashion, frocks such as this change hands for large sums of money in the shops, but are not difficult for someone with a modicum of dressmaking experience to run up. As the pieces are so small, they can be cut from items of adult clothing – a pretty skirt, for instance – that are damaged in places or no longer worn. Using a contrasting or coordinating fabric for the bodice lining and choosing a colourful button from your button tin for the shoulder strap are unusual touches that make each dress unique. The pattern on pages 238–9 can be made up in two sizes to fit an average one- or three-year-old.

You will need

- Pattern from pages 238–9 scaled up on to pattern paper or newspaper
- Main fabric:
  Age 1: 1.1m (43in) x 115cm (45in) wide cotton or 1m (39in) x 152cm (60in) wide cotton
  Age 3: 1.25m (50in) x 115cm (45in) wide cotton or 1m (39in x 152cm (60in) wide cotton
  Lining:
  Ages 1 and 3: 50cm (20in)
  or cut pieces from an old item of clothing
- Cotton thread for machine sewing
- Button from button tin measuring 5mm (¼in) (Age 1) or 1cm (½in) (Age 3)

To make

♥ Cut out the dress pieces as directed on the pattern pieces (these allow to a 1cm (½in) seam throughout), placing the front and back skirt pieces and bodice front (optional) against a fold of fabric. For the bodice, cut two pieces each of front and back, one of fabric and one of lining. Cut two straps (optional). With right sides facing, pin the left shoulder seam of the bodice and sew. Repeat with the bodice lining, sewing the left shoulder seam.

♥ With right sides together, pin the main bodice fabric to the lining, matching up the sewn left shoulder seam. Sew around the left armhole. Beginning at the back right armhole, sew around the back armhole across the shoulder seam, around the neck back and front and around the front armhole.

♥ Trim the seams using sharp scissors and clip around the curved edges to help the bodice lie flat when turned. (You can also machine around the seams using a zigzag stitch to prevent the seams fraying.) Turn to the right side by pulling front through at left shoulder. Iron the seams flat.

♥ For the straps, if using, fold the strap pieces in half lengthwise, right sides together. Sew around the two sides, allowing for a 1cm (½in) seam. Trim the corners, then turn to the right side using a knitting needle, if necessary, to push out the corners. Press with a steam iron.

♥ Pin the straps to the front side seam of the bodice, matching the raw edge of the strap to the side of the bodice, approximately 2cm (¾in) from the bottom edge.

♥ Place the front and back pieces right sides together and matching the underarm seam, and sew the lining side seam, across the underarm seam and then the bodice seam, which catches in the side strap. Repeat on the opposite side.

♥ Make a horizontal buttonhole on the back right shoulder, to fit your button (see pages 226–7). Sew either on the sewing machine or by hand with blanket stitch (see page 225). Sew the button on to the back shoulder.

♥ To make up the skirt, stitch the front to the back side seams. Then make two parallel rows of gathering stitches (long running stitches, see page 226) at the top edge on the front and back to within 1cm (½in) of the side seams. Pull gently to make the gathers the same width as the bodice.

♥ With right sides together, matching side seams with the side seams from the main fabric only, tack the two pieces of the dress together, then sew on or just below the gathering stitches. Trim and finish the join between bodice and skirt with zigzag stitch and press the seam upwards.

♥ Press under the raw edge of the bodice lining by about 1cm (½in) and hand sew with over stitch (see page 226) the folded edge below the stitched line of the gathered skirt to bodice, so hiding the stitch line. Press with a steam iron.

♥ Mark the finished length and trim evenly, allowing about 2cm (¾in) to turn up and press all around. Then press under approximately 5mm (¼in) along the raw edge and stitch the hem either by hand or by machine.

With simple classic childrenswear coming back into fashion, frocks such as these change hands for considerable sums of money in the shops...

Tea towel
apron

SOME TEA TOWELS seem too good for wiping dishes, so why not make one into an apron? This idea is simplicity itself, as it utilizes the ready-finished edges of the tea towel, meaning that there are only a few raw edges to be hemmed. The apron in the photograph was made using a vintage French linen tea towel; you can buy similar ones on eBay or pick them up from antiques markets or junk shops (see Directory, page 242). Any design with an attractive stripe or pattern could be used, though – even a souvenir cloth from a favourite place.

You will need

- Large tea towel measuring 62 x 84cm (24½ x 33in) for an average-sized adult use a smaller one for a child
- White cotton thread
- 2.7m (3yd) cotton tape
- Metal D-ring (optional)

To make

💜 Cut off the top corners of your tea towel so that, when sewn together along their diagonal sides, they form a square. Tea towels vary in size, but for this one, the cuts were made 18cm (7in) in along the top and down each side, leaving 27cm (10½in) (unhemmed) for the neckline.

💜 Turn over the raw edges of the main tea towel twice, press with a steam iron and hem by hand.

💜 To make the pocket, tack together the diagonal sides of the two cut-off triangles, right sides facing, making sure to match any stripes or patterns where you can. Carefully machine stitch together.

💜 Iron out the seam, fold over the raw edges of the pocket square once and hand hem the one that will form the top of the pocket. Pin or tack the pocket into position on the front of the apron and top stitch by machine, finishing securely at all the corners.

💜 To finish, cut the cotton tape into three: two ties of 106cm (42in) each and a neck loop of 60cm (24in). Sew securely into position, using the metal D-ring to make the neck loop adjustable, if required. Press with a steam iron.

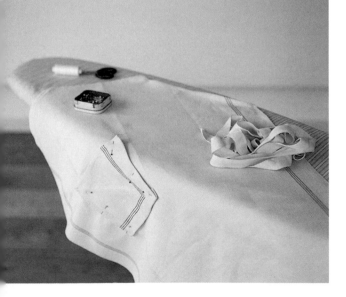

Customizing
T-shirts

CUSTOMIZING T-SHIRTS is enormous fun and can make an enjoyable project for children of all ages. With just a little effort and ingenuity a plain T-shirt can be transformed into a unique and covetable item. You can sew, embroider or appliqué our designs, should you want, but can also be achieved ultra-simply, without sewing – either painting them or using fragments of fabric applied with iron-on webbing. With parental supervision, they would make a great project for a children's birthday party, doing away with the need for a 'going home' present.

You will need

- ◆ A plain T-shirt
- ◆ Pieces of scrap fabric
- ◆ Fusible fabric (such as HeatnBond and Bondaweb, from haberdashery or department stores)

To make

Decide what you want to have on your T-shirt – it could be a name, an image or a slogan; anything is possible. Iron your fabric to the bond paper, then draw your design on to the paper side (remember to reverse the image, if necessary, or the letters if spelling out a name).

♥ Cut out your design, remove the paper backing and simply iron your fabric on to the T-shirt.

Variations

For a painted T-shirt, either you or a child can paint or draw a design on to the T-shirt using fabric paints or fabric crayons (see page 28 for tips on copying images or lettering).

Restoring
a garden table

THE STYLE QUEEN Nancy Lancaster once likened white plastic garden furniture to 'pill packets on a lawn' – and much of the wooden furniture currently available is just as unsightly, not to mention un-ecological. Why buy expensive new items anyway when you can restore old pieces easily enough yourself? You can pick up old metal café tables pretty cheaply from junk shops and antiques fairs – this one was found in a builders' skip, covered in rust.

You will need

- Metal café table in need of restoration
- Stiff wire brush
- Sandpaper or electric hand sander
- Rust-resistant primer
- Paintbrush
- Outdoor eggshell paint (see Directory, page 242)

To make

♥ With the stiff wire brush, remove any loose paint and rusty fragments from the table. Smooth over with sandpaper or, if the top is particularly rusty, use an electric hand sander as the best way to achieve an even surface. Wipe with a damp cloth and leave to dry.

♥ Place the table on old newspapers to catch any drips and treat it with rust-resistant primer – the stuff used for car bodies is fine if you have some spare. Take care to brush into joints, hidden nooks and crannies or decorative features. Leave the primer to dry.

♥ Give the table a lick of paint. Two coats of outdoor eggshell should be enough to give it a good finish. Choose a colour that complements the paintwork of your house as well as the planting in your garden – soft greys, off-whites and blue-greens all look good outside.

♥ Paint other pieces of old furniture in the same colour or use varying shades in the same tonal range.

Renovating a garden chair

OLD CRICKET CHAIRS are ideal for garden seating because they are light enough to move about easily and can be folded up and stored away when not needed. They can be picked up cheaply at junk shops and antiques fairs and restored without too much trouble or expense. It is worth building up a collection, keeping a few out year round and stashing the rest in the shed to bring out for an alfresco lunch or party. Don't worry if they're not exactly the same – painting a motley mix of shapes and sizes all the same colour will have a unifying effect. Or if you are lucky enough to find a matching set, from an old school or bandstand, perhaps, try painting them in different shades of the same colour-group – smoky blue-greys and mauves, for instance, or olive green through grey-greens to brown. Padded cushions tied on to the frame (see overleaf) stylishly complete the effect.

You will need

- Cricket chair in need of renovation
- Stiff wire brush
- Fine sandpaper
- Rust-resistant primer
- Paintbrush
- Wood glue
- Outdoor eggshell paint (see Directory, page 242)

To make

♥ With the stiff wire brush, remove any loose paint and rusty fragments from the chair and then smooth down using fine sandpaper. Wipe with a damp cloth and leave to dry.

♥ Place the chair on old newspapers to catch any drips and treat any rusty metal parts with rust-resistant primer. Take care to brush into joints, hidden nooks and crannies or decorative features. Leave the primer to dry.

♥ Check the wooden parts for hardiness and, where necessary, repair any cracked back slats or other small areas of damage with wood glue.

♥ When dry, give the chair two coats of outdoor eggshell paint, taking care to brush along the undersides of the slats and into any other hidden-away areas. You may have to touch up the chair slightly in places where the folding mechanism gets in the way.

Outdoor tie-on
cushion

GIVE OLD CRICKET CHAIRS (see page 80) or other garden seating a lift with smart tie-on fabric cushions. Choose a hardwearing material, such as canvas, striped ticking or even oilcloth (see Directory, pages 242–4) in a pattern and shade that goes well with the colour of your furniture, as well as the flowers in your garden. A mismatch of various vintage fabrics looks lovely, so raid your scrap box for possibilities. For the ties, you can buy cotton tape from haberdashery counters, but the paper carrier bags given away free in many shops often have tape handles in attractive colours that can be removed and saved for such a purpose (see also Wrapping presents on page 206).

You will need

- ◆ Cushion pad or thick foam cut to size
- ◆ Hardwearing fabric (see above)
- ◆ Sewing thread to match fabric
- ◆ 80cm (32in) tape or ribbon

To make

♥ This cushion has an envelope-style opening like the one on page 135. Cut three pieces of fabric: one the size of your cushion plus a 2cm (¾in) seam allowance (Piece A) and two that each measure two-thirds of the length of the cushion plus seam allowance (Pieces B and C). Pieces B and C will ultimately overlap each other on the back of the cushion to form the opening for inserting the pad. You may want to cut out Piece C with the selvedge forming the open edge.

♥ Hem the unfinished edge of B that will form part of the opening (and C, too, if you haven't made use of the selvedge).

♥ Cut four lengths of tape or ribbon 20cm (8in) long each for the ties.

♥ Lay out your pieces with Piece A on the bottom (right side facing up), followed by Pieces B and then C on top (right sides facing down) so that they overlap, pinning two ties between the layers of fabric at each of two adjacent corners so that the ends of the ties are trapped between the seams.

♥ Sew around the four sides. Turn the cushion cover out so the right side is visible, iron the seams flat, insert the cushion pad and use the ties to attach to the back of the chair.

Recycled
containers

USING RECYCLED CONTAINERS is a great way to bring individual style to your garden, without costing the earth. From large wooden tea crates to old wicker baskets down to tiny biscuit tins, there are containers of every size, type and material just waiting to be given a new lease of life as planters. It is all a matter of seeing things with new eyes: could that old metal dustbin cast out on the street by a neighbour become home to a small apple tree on an urban terrace or balcony? Could that holey old watering can be planted up with white petunias? Even toy trucks and boats can be planted up with shallow-rooted plants, such as succulents, to bring a quirky touch to a children's play area. Take inspiration from thrifty gardeners in Greece, India and Cuba and plant olive trees in large empty olive oil cans or use everything from old buckets to chipped china as containers for edible or ornamental plants. (See Directory, page 242 for places to find salvaged containers.)

Late summer fireworks

Old fire buckets (see opposite) are a great choice for the hot fiery colours of late summer flowers, such as dahlias, crocosmias and heleniums, offset by dark and bronzy ornamental grasses. Some of the buckets are rounded at the bottom, so you can use the handle to turn them into smart hanging baskets. Unless they are really rusty, the buckets may need to have extra drainage holes made in the base.

Seaside special

Paint old tyres and use them as containers – or why not use a container made from recycled rubber, such as this one (see right)? Given good drainage and planted up with sun-loving plants like ornamental grasses, small scabious and thrift (*Armeria maritima*), a container like this is perfect for a seaside garden or an exposed urban roof terrace, where the grasses can swish about in the wind.

Take inspiration from thrifty gardeners in Greece, India and Cuba and plant olive trees in large, empty olive oil cans...

A mismatch of found and recycled objects (see right) can look charming in a garden. But if the make-do-and-mend aesthetic isn't what you had in mind, don't worry. Giving a motley collection of objects a coat of paint in a unifying colour will instantly make them look much smarter, and it's up to you whether you choose a bright indigo blue, such as that in Yves Saint Laurent's famous Majorelle Gardens in Morocco, or lower-key grey-greens and blues.

The good news is that recycled objects often already have ready-made drainage holes in the form of rust holes, gaps and cracks. If they don't have sufficient drainage, the plants won't thrive, so carefully knock or drill more holes, using masking tape around the hole to protect more delicate materials. If metal pots, such as buckets, have a lot of rust, treat them with rust-resistant primer first (see page 78 for instructions). If edible plants are to be grown in the pots, it is advisable to line them first (see page 50 for instructions). Then fill base of the containers with at least 2.5cm (1in) of gravel to further improve drainage and provide some weight for anchoring lighter pots in place.

Pineapple lily

An old florist's bucket (opposite) makes a great vase-like container for the unusual late-summer blooms of the pineapple lily (*Eucomis bicolor*). Drill a few holes for drainage in the base of the bucket and fill the bottom with 15cm (6in) of gravel – vital for anchoring tall planters such as this in place. A mulch of grit, gravel or shells on top of the soil keeps weeds down and water in.

Tomato box

Why grow tomato plants in boring black plastic pots when a recycled wooden tomato box (see left) is just as effective and twice as much fun? This is a vintage box, but attractive new ones can be picked up from street markets. Line the box with black plastic to retain soil and water (see page 50), place in a sunny spot and keep well fed and watered.

Tea for two

An old enamel teapot and caddy and a chipped china jug have been given new life (see left) as planters for flowering verbenas in crimson and mauve. When using a mixture of containers, it often looks smarter to restrict the planting to one or two types of flowers or colours. Old enamelware makes great planters and can often be picked up cheaply if there are rust patches – just drill or hammer a few extra holes in the base.

Drought-proof trough

An unwanted galvanized water-tank makes a witty container for drought-proof plants (see below), which won't need much watering in hot spells. Combine yellow red-hot pokers (*Kniphofia citrina*) and electric purple *Verbena bonariensis* with creamy heads of achillea as a contrasting horizontal shape. Silvery leaves of lavender at the base are the perfect complement for the weathered grey metal of the tank. This would probably need more drainage holes drilled in the base before use. A mulch of pebbles retains water well.

Mexican
tin lantern

INSPIRED BY THIS wonderful Mexican tin lantern that was a present from a friend (see below), here is a less elaborate, but nevertheless charming, version to make yourself. A string of such lanterns, either lined up along a wall or hung from the branches of a tree, would look fabulous. The pinpricks of light cast lovely shadows, while the tin provides the candle with protection from the wind. For a special birthday, wedding or anniversary party you could even punch out names, initials or a personal message.

You will need

- ◆ An empty tin can, washed out and label and lid removed
- ◆ Erasable felt pen
- ◆ Bradawl or small screwdriver
- ◆ Hammer
- ◆ Wire for handle
- ◆ Night-light

To make

♥ The lantern illustrated uses a standard size can, but smaller and larger sizes work well too. It is possible to make the holes directly with a bradawl and hammer, but the following method makes it easier and safer to work with.

♥ Fill the can with water and place it in the freezer until the water has frozen. Then draw your design on the can with an erasable felt pen. Abstract designs like crosses and zigzags work well as borders, with stars and hearts or even birds or flowers as features around the central body of the can.

♥ Lay the can on to a non-slip surface, such as a towel, and wedge it in position by rolling the towel towards the can on either sade. Alternatively, place in a vice, but be careful not to squeeze it out of shape. Using a large nail or bradawl, hammer holes into the can following your design. Place the finished frozen can into the sink to thaw.

♥ To make a hanging lantern, punch an additional hole on either side near the rim and add a wire handle, twisting to secure in place.

♥ Place a night-light in the base of the tin. For added safety, particularly if the lantern is going to sit on a wooden or heat-sensitive surface, sit the night-light on a small tile or flat fragment of slate or ceramic. Keep an eye on your lantern when lit, and never leave it unattended.

Paper-lined night-light
holders

WHY WASTE MONEY on fancy tea-light holders for the garden when you can make your own stylish versions from recycled jam jars decorated with old wrapping paper torn into strips, or handmade papers from craft shops (see Directory, page 242)? Get into the habit of saving useful jam jars and experiment with textured Japanese papers that tear to leave an irregular edge, as shown here, or ones that incorporate pressed flowers or skeleton leaves. Papers with a see-through texture or cutout motif work best.

You will need

- Clean, empty jam jars of assorted sizes
- Strips of recycled or handmade paper
- Glue or sticky tape
- Wire or ribbon for handles
- Night-lights

To make

♥ Cut or tear a strip of handmade craft paper to fit the circumference of each jar, wrap it around the outside of the jar and secure in place using strong glue or sticky tape.

♥ For handles, bend wire around the rim of the jar and over the top, twisting securely in place. Or use coloured narrow ribbon, as here, tying it around the rim, extending one end of the ribbon in a loop over the top and securing it in a double knot on the other side.

♥ Pop a night-light inside and hang the jars from a pergola or the branches of a tree, making sure there is no foliage directly above the lanterns that could get burnt. Never leave lit lanterns unattended.

Variations

For a variation, cut your own designs from tracing paper and stick them around the jar or paint the glass with glass paint. Threading beads on wire and slipping over the neck of the jar makes a pretty collar.

Experiment with textured Japanese papers that tear to leave an irregular edge.

Summer
bunting

STRUNG FROM LEAFY BRANCHES and blowing gently in a warm breeze, fabric bunting brings a festive air to the summer garden. Good times are here, it seems to say – suggesting parties, village fêtes and wholesome fun and games. Making your own is much easier than you would think – and means you will always have instant decorations to hand. It's yet another great way to use up odd small remnants of fabric and much-loved old clothes. Make it as long as you like, or sew several lengths to be used in different places. Bunting looks beautiful indoors as well as out, looped along verandahs, draped across doorways or hung in swags around the walls of a child's bedroom year-round. If you are a member of a craft club, why not make lots of bunting as a communal project and lend it out to each other for parties as required? This bunting is machine-washable and is best kept folded flat in a box between uses to prevent it getting tangled.

You will need

- A mixture of plain, striped and floral cotton fabrics
- 16m (17½yd) coloured tape or binding a minimum of 2cm (¾in) wide

To make

♥ Using pinking shears (so that you don't have to hem each piece), cut out 50 triangles, each measuring 22cm (8½in) wide and deep. Decide on the order of your coloured triangles, aiming to get a good mix of patterns and colours.

♥ Fold the tape in half lengthwise and iron to make a long channel for inserting the triangles.

♥ Starting about 20cm (8in) in from the end of the tape (to leave some free for tying), pin the triangles in position, 10cm (4in) apart, opening up the tape and slipping the top of each triangle inside so the raw edge is hidden. Stop 20cm (8in) short of the other end of the tape.

♥ Machine carefully into place all along the length of the tape to secure the triangles in place.

♥ Making a loop at either end can make hanging easier – and extra tape can be added to extend the bunting or to make it easier to tie on to trees and so on.

Bag-in-a-bag

PLASTIC CARRIER BAGS are a definite no-no in both the eco-conscious and the style stakes. But finding the right shopping bag – one that's big and strong enough to carry heavy groceries, light enough to fold up small and fit in your handbag and stylish to boot – is like searching for the Holy Grail. The one featured here ticks all the right boxes, incorporating a gusset for extra capacity and a pretty ribbon and button tie for rolling it up small. It's also surprisingly simple to make – choose from striped cotton canvas or pink metallic nylon for a touch of glamour.

You will need

- 1m (39in) in any standard width of strong fabric that isn't too thick or heavy; or use an off-cut measuring 64 x 80cm (25 x 32in)
- Cotton thread for machine sewing
- 20–30cm (8–12in) ribbon
- A pretty button

To make

♥ For the bag, cut out a piece of fabric measuring 80 x 46cm (32 x 18in) – including a 1.5cm (½in) seam allowance.

♥ To make the straps, cut two strips of fabric, each measuring 54 x 9cm (21 x 3½in). Fold in 5mm (¼in) on each side to the wrong side and iron flat. Then fold each strap in half lengthwise (so that the pattern is on the outside and the folded edges are facing inwards), and machine topstitch all the way along.

♥ For the top edge of the bag, fold in one of the longer sides by 3mm (⅛in) to the wrong side. Iron in place and then fold down a further 4cm (1½in) and iron again.

♥ Pin the two handles in place, beginning with handle one about 10cm (4in) in from the right side edge. Pin one end of the handle, then pin the opposite end about 13cm (54in) away from the first end. Have the stitches on the inner side of the handles, and the bottom of the strap pieces level with the bottom of the folded-over edge of the bag (see top picture on page 99). Repeat at the opposite end with handle two.

♥ Secure the handles in place and stitch down the top of the bag with two rows of machine stitching, one about 3mm (⅛in) from the top edge and the other along the bottom of the folded-over edge (see top right).

♥ Fold the bag in half, right sides together. Sew the side and bottom seams about 1.5cm (½in) in from the edge. Zigzag stitch over the raw edges to prevent fraying.

♥ To make the gusset, open the bag out so the bottom seam runs down the centre and sew a diagonal line of about 10cm (4in) across each corner (see below right).

♥ To make the ribbon and button tie, loop the length of ribbon around one of the handles, joining and securing with a button (see left).

♥ To roll up the bag, fold it into three or four sections and roll up, leaving the straps end until last. Then simply wrap the ribbon tie around the roll and wind the loose end of the ribbon around the button to secure.

Finding the right shopping bag is like searching for the Holy Grail...

Beach bag

A GOOD-LOOKING yet practical bag makes a trip to the beach all the more enjoyable. Wider than the shopping bag on page 96 and with longer straps, this bag has been designed to take a large towel and bathing suit, plus picnic goodies, tubes of sun lotion, books, a hat and other holiday paraphernalia. Lining the inside with towelling makes the bag extra useful for carrying damp swimsuits back from the beach. We used an old towel that still had plenty of wear left in it but was a bit frayed around the edges. With enough left over, you could also line the shoulder straps with towelling to make them more comfortable. The instructions for the beach bag are similar to those for the shopping bag, but the dimensions are different.

You will need

◆ 1.2m (1¼yd) in any standard width of strong cotton or canvas-type fabric (we used gingham); or use an off-cut measuring 115 x 70cm (45 x 28in)
◆ Towelling: same size as the main fabric – an old towel would be perfect
◆ Cotton thread for machine sewing
◆ Tapestry wool
◆ Recycled rope, shells and anything else you have to hand, to decorate

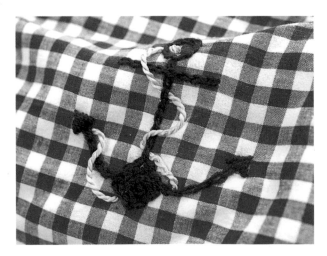

To make

♥ For the bag, cut two pieces measuring 115 x 50cm (45 x 20in), one in the main fabric and the other in the towelling. Place wrong sides together and use as a single piece, tacking together if necessary.

♥ For the straps, cut two strips of the main fabric, each measuring 95 x 10cm (27½ x 4in).

♥ Make up the bag using the instructions for the Bag-in-a-bag on page 96.

♥ To decorate, stitch an anchor (see page 240) or other seaside image on to your bag using chain stitch (see page 225). We used tapestry wool rather than embroidery thread as wool really stands out, and then added a rope-like piece of trimming recycled from a carrier bag. Add shells and other beachcombing finds, strung like fashionable chains or trophies from the straps (see the Beach sculpture or mobile overleaf for further inspiration).

Beach sculpture or mobile

BEACHCOMBING IS A GREAT pastime, especially for those people who find it hard to sit still. Quite apart from the fact that it is not often hot enough in Britain to lie and bake in the sun, many people find it hard to remain still and would far rather be doing something creative with their time. The rhythm of the tides is endlessly fascinating, and a walk along the shoreline at low tide can be both relaxing and inspiring as the sea breezes blow any worries away, while the flotsam and jetsam may well provide ideas for things to make.

Everyone from toddlers upwards seems to collect buckets or pockets full of seaside finds, so why not make something beautiful or useful with them, rather than leaving them lying around the house gathering dust? This beach sculpture or mobile was made from beachcombings from Cornwall and was inspired by something similar made from shells and lengths of fishing wire by Ros's brother, Mike Badger. Follow the instructions given below, or go on your own tack, inspired by whatever you find. The result is now hanging on the sitting room wall as a permanent reminder of a great summer holiday.

You will need
◆ Shells and stones with holes through them (limpet shells with the pointy tops knocked off them are often found in rocky coves and bays, or tiny white conches that look lovely grouped on a table at home)
◆ A length of fishing line (we found one washed up with the decorative sparkly flies still attached)
◆ A piece of driftwood

To make
♥ Tie a knot in one end of the fishing line and thread on the shells in whatever order works best for you.

♥ When the shell chain is long enough, tie a knot in the other end of the line to secure your finds and attach to a length of driftwood.

Variations

This could also be used as a bell or light pull (see instructions for the Button light pull on page 168). To make a beach mobile, tie small groups of shells on to lengths of rope or fishing line (preferably beachcombed) and hang from either end of a piece of driftwood. This would look particularly good in a beach hut.

Other uses for beachcombing finds include the Razor shell candleholders on page 124.

Moroccan mint tea

MAKING FRESH MINT TEA as they do in Morocco is a great pleasure in summer. Not only is the minty taste delicious and refreshing, it can also have a calming effect on the stomach, and so is good for serving after an alfresco lunch or supper. Using pretty painted tea glasses, silver trays and teapots all adds to the ritual. A plentiful supply of mint is essential, so plant a large patch in a corner of your garden or allotment, or keep some in a big planter. Remember, though, that mint is incredibly invasive: retaining the roots (even in a large pot buried in the open ground) will prevent it taking over! Keep it well watered in dry weather and protect from hungry slugs and snails, who will strip the stalks in no time.

To make the tea, take a good sprig of ten or so leaves of mint, place in the bottom of a tea glass and crush slightly with a pestle (or spoon) to release the flavour and aroma. Add a spoonful of sugar or honey to taste, before pouring on boiling water – the Moroccans do this in a teapot from a great height to aerate the tea and improve the taste.

Variations on a mint theme

Adding mint leaves, fresh lemon slices and ice cubes to a glass jug of water is a simple yet refreshing touch. Or, for a minty summer cocktail, make mojitos – as enjoyed by Ernest Hemingway in Havana – by placing 6–8 fresh mint leaves in the bottom of a tumbler and crushing slightly with a pestle before adding one part freshly squeezed lime juice to two parts white rum, sugar to taste and topping up with sparkling water.

Summer salad
trough

YOU DON'T HAVE to have an allotment to grow your own food – a windowsill or even a sunny spot on an outdoor table will do. This recycled metal pig trough makes a great container, and is filled with plants that taste and smell as good as they look. Growing the strawberries off the ground like this helps protect them from hungry slugs and snails, allowing them to ripen quickly in the sun. The different species of basil, mint and sage that have been used add colour and aroma to the mix – chocolate mint goes well with strawberries, while some people swear by basil to bring out the flavour of the fruit. Threaded throughout, jaunty 'Jackanapes' violas not only pick up the burgundy in the leaves of the basil but can also be eaten. For an unusual and attractive pudding, pick your strawberries, choose a herb to chop or tear over the fruit and sprinkle with sugar and viola leaves.

You will need

- ◆ A salvaged pig trough or other small window box
- ◆ Black bin liner or compost bag (optional)
- ◆ Gravel
- ◆ General-purpose potting compost
- ◆ 5 large strawberry plants
- ◆ 3 mint or sage plants – here chocolate mint, lime mint and tangerine sage
- ◆ 3 viola 'Jackanapes' or similar
- ◆ 3 purple-leafed basil plants

To make

♥ Line the planter if necessary (see page 50) and then add a 5cm (2in) drainage layer of gravel to the base of the trough. Add compost until the soil in the tallest pots is level with the top of the trough.

♥ Knock the plants gently out of their pots, then line the strawberry plants along the front and shorter sides of the trough and fill in with herbs and flowers in a roughly symmetrical arrangement. Add more compost between the plants so that everything is firmly bedded in.

♥ Keep the soil moist for juicy fruit and luscious leaves – this may mean watering every day in hot spells.

♥ Provide extra slug protection by standing the trough on sheets of sandpaper or special slug-proof mats.

Colourful cupcakes

There is something very cheering about cupcakes, whether beautifully decorated like those in stylish bakeries, or studded with Smarties by creative kids. Having the ingredients for a basic recipe up your sleeve can provide you with something instant for when friends or relatives turn up unexpectedly; equally they can be a fun rainy-day project for children, and a great last-minute present idea. Bake in advance for a children's party or picnic and let the children decorate their own; line up on a tray and spell out 'HAPPY BIRTHDAY', 'ANNIVERSARY' or so on, plus the recipient's name; or pack in a pretty box or tin tied up with ribbon, which can form part of the present. The following recipe, which can be made by hand or using a hand-held electric whisk, makes 12 regular-sized cakes. For a professional finish, try not to overfill the cases; the icing looks better if contained by the paper cases rather than dripping down the sides. There are endless variations for decorating the cakes – see right and overleaf for some ideas.

You will need

- 110g (4oz) butter, softened
- 110g (4oz) caster sugar
- 2 large eggs
- 1 tsp vanilla essence
- 110g (4oz) self-raising flour, sifted
- 1 tsp baking powder
- 200g (7oz) icing sugar
- Juice of 1 lemon
- Food colouring (optional)
- Assorted sugar balls, flowers, sweets and so on, to decorate

To make

♥ Preheat the oven to 170°C (325°F), Gas 3. Line a 12-hole muffin tin with cupcake cases.

♥ Put the butter and sugar in a bowl and, either whisking by hand or using a hand-held electric whisk, cream together until light and fluffy. Beat the eggs in a separate bowl and add to the mixture gradually, along with the vanilla essence. Fold in the flour and baking powder and mix gently together. Spoon into the cases, leaving room for the cakes to rise.

♥ Bake for 20–25 minutes until the tops are golden and firm to the touch. Remove and allow to cool before decorating.

♥ To make the icing, sift the icing sugar into a bowl and beat in the lemon juice until smooth. Divide into smaller bowls and add colouring, if using, one drop at a time, until the desired shade is reached. Spoon on to the cakes and decorate as much or as little as you want.

There is something very cheering about cupcakes, whether beautifully decorated like those in stylish bakeries, or studded with Smarties by creative kids.

Foolproof strawberry
jam

MAKING JAM CAN be gloriously satisfying. It's a great way to use up piles of perishable soft fruit from the garden, farmers' market or pick-your-own farm. As you pour the jewel-bright mixture into jars, you can feel as if you are preserving the very essence of summer to enjoy in the winter months ahead – provided you can wait that long! But the process can also be plagued by pitfalls, leaving you hot and bad-tempered with a gloopy mess that refuses to set or a stiff goo that cuts like jelly – never anything in between. The following recipe should ensure success every time, however. Using jam sugar for low-pectin fruits such as strawberries definitely helps, as does heating the sugar in the oven first, which reduces the overall cooking time. Slow cooking before the sugar is added and a very intense and short boil afterwards preserves the colour and flavour of the fruit as well as providing the best consistency.

You will need

- 1.5kg (3lb 6oz) strawberries, wiped clean and with the stalks removed
- Juice of 1 large lemon
- 2kg (4lb 8oz) jam sugar, heated for 20 minutes in a low oven
- Knob of butter
- 5 x 375g (13oz) sterilized jars

To make

♥ Put a small plate in the fridge to cool. Place the fruit and lemon juice in a stainless steel (aluminium can react with acid fruit) preserving pan and heat until the juices run. Crush with a potato masher and cook for a further 5 minutes without boiling.

♥ Add the warmed sugar and stir until completely dissolved, still being careful not to boil. Add the butter. Then, increase the heat to maximum and bring to a full rolling boil that cannot be stirred down. Start timing and boil for 4 minutes.

♥ Remove from the heat and test whether it has set by dropping a teaspoonful of jam on the chilled plate, leaving for a minute and seeing if wrinkles form when the surface is pushed with a spoon. If they do, the jam is ready and can be poured into sterilized jars (fresh from a hot dishwasher will do), labelled and stored. If not, boil up again and test a few minutes later.

♥ If giving your jam away as presents, make pretty cotton covers and secure them with string or an elastic band. Using a print featuring the fruit you have used is a nice touch – this one (see right) was found on eBay.

As you pour the jewel-bright mixture into jars, you can feel as if you are preserving the very essence of summer to enjoy in the winter months ahead...

Fresh-baked
scones

THE WONDERFUL THING about scones is that the minimal effort involved is far, far outweighed by the pleasure they give. Unlike homemade bread, which can take ages to make and is often not a great deal better than a loaf bought from a good baker's, homemade scones are immeasurably superior to anything that can be found in the shops. This is because, to be enjoyed at their peak, they have to be eaten on the day they are made, ideally still slightly warm. Serve with whipped or clotted cream and homemade jam (see page 116). Keep the ingredients permanently in your larder and you'll never be at a loss to feed unexpected teatime guests in style!

NB Many recipes specify plain flour, but using self-raising flour instead ensures lovely deep scones with a light, fluffy texture. This recipe makes about 8 large scones.

You will need

- ◆ 225g (8oz) self-raising flour, plus extra for dusting
- ◆ 40g (1½oz) caster sugar
- ◆ 75g (3oz) butter, cold and diced, plus extra for greasing
- ◆ 300ml (½ pint) milk, plus extra for glazing
- ◆ 1 egg, beaten

To make

♥ Preheat the oven to 220°C (425°F), Gas 7. Lightly grease a baking sheet and dust with flour. Sift the flour into a large bowl, stir in the sugar and then rub in the butter until the mixture resembles damp sand. Add the milk and egg and mix briefly to bring it together.

♥ Turn out on to a floured surface and knead lightly to form a dough. Roll out to a thickness of at least 2.5cm (1in) – this is the secret of well-risen scones. Cut out the scones using crinkle-edged round cutters (about 6.5cm (2½in) in diameter is a good size) and place on the baking sheet.

♥ Brush the scones lightly with a little milk and then dust them with flour. Bake in the oven for 10–12 minutes, or until they are well risen and golden brown. Remove them to a wire rack to cool.

Variations

For fruit scones, add 75g (3oz) raisins, sultanas or chopped dried sour cherries and the grated zest of half an orange.
For a savoury version, replace the sugar with 75g (3oz) grated Cheddar cheese and serve sandwiched with unsalted butter and fresh cress.

Razor shell
candleholders

THE IDEA FOR THESE lovely shell candleholders came from a friend, Carolyn Brookes-Davies of the hat shop Fred Bare, who lives near the beach in Norfolk. The natural colours of the shells are beautiful, and turn translucent as the candles burn down inside. For more ideas using natural objects, see the Beach sculpture or mobile on page 102 and the Artichoke candleholders on page 130.

You will need (per candle)

◆ At least 20 razor shells – the more, the better
◆ A tall candle (such as a church candle)
◆ Twine, string or raffia

To make

♥ Gather empty razor shells, which can often be found in abundance along British beaches at low tide. Wash them well in soapy water to remove any salt, slime or seaweed.

♥ Take a tall candle, either standard size or wider if you wish – the parchment-coloured 'church' candles tend to look best and burn well. Holding it upright on a flat surface, gather the shells, curved side outwards, around it until the base of the candle is well covered all the way around.

♥ Tie tightly in place with attractive twine, string or raffia and stand on an old saucer. Keep a constant eye on your candleholders once lit.

The shells turn translucent as the candles burn down inside...

Empty razor shells can often be found in abundance along British beaches at low tide...

Pumpkin
lanterns

PUMPKIN LANTERNS DON'T have to have ghoulish grins and angular eyes. Let your imagination lead you to other attractive designs that are not so associated with Hallowe'en and can be used to bring a warm golden glow to other autumnal festivities. Try piercing swirly patterns with a skewer, in the style of the Mexican tin lantern on page 90, or go for simpler, more geometric patterns such as those shown here. The polka-dot effect was created using an apple corer, which passes easily through the tough skin and flesh of a pumpkin, and the stars in the lid were cut using a sharp kitchen knife.

All a-glow

Creating the lantern itself can be part of the fun, especially if you've grown them yourself. A fine crop of pumpkins is a good excuse for an autumn party, and children will enjoy choosing their own pumpkin and carving out a design with an adult's help. The scooping can be hard work, however, and is best done with a metal spoon with sharp sides; save the pulp to make soup or chutney, and the seeds for toasting in a low oven – as snacks or for sprinkling on salads or flapjacks – or for sowing next spring.

Light the finished lanterns and arange in a row along the top of a wall or porch steps until it is time for them to be carefully cradled home. Three night-lights to each lantern give a warm flickering glow. A cluster of these lanterns in a variety of different designs adds immeasurably to the atmosphere of any gathering, inside or out. Take care to site holes in the lid directly above the candle flames, or you will get roasted pumpkin – and never leave lit lanterns unattended.

A *fine* crop of pumpkins is a
good excuse for an autumn party.

Artichoke candleholders

USING NATURAL OBJECTS around the home brings indoors the beauty and energy of the beach, garden or countryside. These simple yet stylish candleholders are a great way to exhibit beachcombing finds or gone-to-seed artichoke heads from the garden or allotment. Inspired by a similar holder made by Francine Raymond of The Kitchen Garden (see Directory, page 250), they take just a moment or two to make, but are so beautiful you'll be sure to get endless comments about them. Cardoons, which are similar to artichokes, also work well. These look great in a line or cluster on a dinner table, where the dried-out heads are illuminated to a lovely old gold by the night-light inside.

You will need (per candle)

- Cardoon or artichoke head
- Night-light
- Small tile or fragment of ceramic

To make

♥ Gather some globe artichoke or cardoon heads that have flowered and gone to seed – the larger the better.

♥ Remove each internal 'choke' by simply pulling out the fluffy seeds to leave a hollow receptacle surrounded by the dried scaly calyxes.

♥ Pop a small tile or flat fragment of slate or ceramic in the bottom of each artichoke to provide some extra heat resistance, and place a night-light on top.

♥ Keep an eye on your candleholders once lit and never leave them unattended.

These look great in a line on a dinner table, where the dried-out heads are illuminated to a lovely old gold by the night-light inside.

Cushion
covers

WHY BUY EXPENSIVE cushion covers when they are dead easy to make and a great way to use up odd pieces of fabric? The ones piled up in the picture use everything from vintage silk scarves to worn linen curtains, an old cable-stitch cotton jersey and an unwanted woollen blanket. Part of the fun lies in choosing and matching the fabrics. The instructions overleaf are for the blanket cover, where the front and back are in the same material, but using a contrasting colour or texture for each side can look very stylish, and allows you to change the look of your room or sofa in an instant simply by turning over the cushions. For instance, the silk scarf cushion at the bottom of the pile has a back made from luxurious soft pink velvet, chosen to pick out one of the colours in the floral pattern. Try mixing knitted cotton or linen (from an old summer jersey) with a woven linen stripe, felted cashmere with slub silk, or even suede (from the back of an old jacket) with sheepskin or sequins.

Be sure to use a machine stitch that suits both fabrics (if using more than one) without pulling, or sew together (right sides facing) by hand. The instructions given overleaf show how to make an envelope opening, but if you want a 'two-sided' cushion, make the cover in three pieces (see instructions for the Outdoor tie-on cushion on page 82, omitting the ties), sew up by hand at one end and unpick for washing.

Recycling blankets

The blanket cushion cover is a good way of using an unwanted blanket (or large jersey) or one that has been stained or damaged in parts. If it's been moth eaten, kill off any remaining moths or eggs by dry cleaning or leaving overnight in the freezer. If there is a stripe or pattern in the blanket, work out where you would like this on the cushion. You can also make use of edges already finished in blanket stitch or ribbon edging.

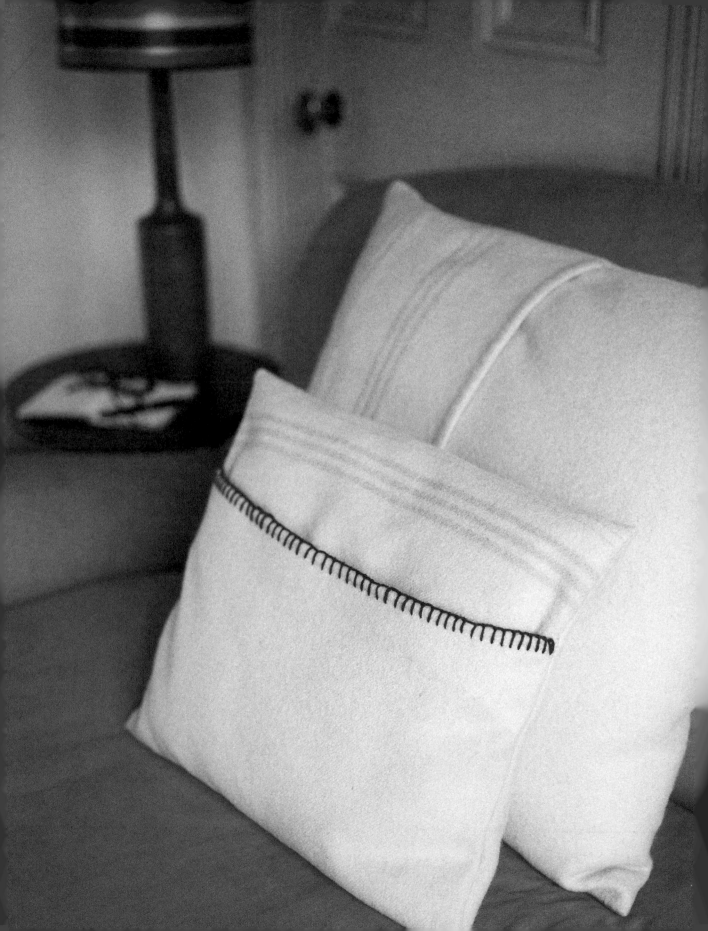

Try mixing knitted cotton or linen (from an old summer jersey) with a woven linen stripe, felted cashmere with slub silk, or even suede (from the back of an old jacket) with sheepskin or sequins.

You will need

- An old blanket or large sweater
- Cushion pad
- Wool for blanket stitch (optional)
- Strong cotton thread for machine sewing
- Buttons or tapes for opening (optional)

To make

♥ Starting from a finished edge, cut a length of fabric two-and-a-half times longer than the cushion pad, plus 2.5cm (1in) all around to allow for seams. Hem any unfinished edges or fold over and edge with blanket stitch (see page 225).

♥ Fold the fabric, right sides together, as if wrapping around a cushion, so that the edge that you want visible for the outer side of the envelope come two-thirds of the way up the length of the cushion. Make sure, too, that this edge is inside, facing downwards, with the other flap over the top.

♥ Machine or hand stitch securely along the two outside edges of the cover, sewing through two and then three layers of fabric. Turn the cover inside out, iron if required and insert the cushion pad.

♥ Sew on buttons or tapes to fasten the opening if required.

iPod cover

IPOD COVERS are all the rage and are sold for high prices in the shops. But it is easy for even novice knitters to make their own and customize to their own designs. These make great presents for both sexes and all ages; simply vary the colour and design to suit. The instructions below include an optional crocheted strap, but if you don't know how to crochet, a pretty piece of ribbon would work just as well.

You will need

- 4-ply cotton, approximately 10g (½oz) (we used mercerized cotton, which has a slight sheen and washes well)
- 2.75mm (UK size 12; US size 2) knitting needles
- 2.5mm crochet hook

Tension over stocking stitch

16sts and 22 rows = 5cm (2in)

Abbreviations

See page 229

Measurements

7 x 8.5cm (2¾ x 3½in)

To make an iPod nano cover

♥ With 2.75mm (UK size 12; US size 2) needles and the 4-ply cotton, cast on 22sts and work 8 rows in garter st (knit every row) then work in stocking st (knit one row, purl one row) until the cover measures 15cm (6in).
Work 8 rows garter st and cast off.
Fold the bag in half, right sides together, sew the two side seams and then turn through.

To make an iPod classic or other MP3 player cover

♥ Measure your player and, using the tension guide (see left), work out how many sts you need for the width, then add 4 more sts.

♥ With 2.75mm (UK size 12; US size 2) needles, cast on the required number of sts and work 8 rows garter st, then work in stocking st until the piece measures twice the length of your player.
Work 8 more rows of garter st and cast off.
Fold the bag in half, right sides together, sew the two side seams and then turn through.

To make the strap

♥ With 2.5mm crochet hook and the 4-ply cotton, make a 30cm (12in) long single chain.

♥ Thread this through the knitted bag just below the garter st top. Alternatively, thread through with narrow ribbon. There is no need to make eyelet holes as the chain st/ribbon can easily be threaded through between the knitted sts. Tie together the loose ends to make a loop.

Tea
cosy

As WELL AS keeping your tea hot, a homemade tea cosy brings an air of warmth and originality to the kitchen table. Choose colours that work with your cups and kitchen décor. For added quirkiness, substitute the embroidered teacup for a message such as 'DRINK ME', 'AAAAH!' or 'THE BEST DRINK OF THE DAY'.

You will need
- About 60g (2¼oz) yarn (this was knitted using Aran tweed but any Aran yarn would also work), plus scraps in contrasting colours for the embroidery and pompom
- 4.5mm (UK size 7; US size 7) needles (you can change the needle size to make the cosy larger or smaller; the one pictured fits a six-teacup teapot)

Tension
10sts and 12 rows = 5cm (2in)

Abbreviations
See page 229

To make
♥ With 4.5mm (UK size 7; US size 7) needles and yarn, cast on 84sts and work 5 rows to form the border.

Row 1: Knit.
Row 2: Purl.
Repeat these 2 rows once more then divide (work for spout and handle).
Row 5: K42 and keep remaining sts on a stitch holder.
Row 6: K2, p38, k2.

Repeat the last 2 rows 10 times more, ending on a purl row.
Keep these sts on a stitch holder and repeat on the opposite side until the work measures the same front and back. End on a purl row.
Next row: Knit across the whole work.
Next row: Purl.

Then start decreasing as follows:
Row 1: K11, k2tog, * k12, k2tog *, repeat from * to * 5 times, k1. (78sts)
Row 2: Purl.
Row 3: K10, k2tog, * k11, k2tog *, repeat from * to * 5 times, k1. (72sts)
Row 4: Purl.
Row 5: K9, k2tog, * k10, k2tog *, repeat from * to * 5 times, k1. (66sts)
Row 6: Purl.
Row 7: K8, k2tog, * k9, k2tog *, repeat from * to * 5 times, k1. (60sts)
Row 8: Purl.
Row 9: K7, k2tog, * k8, k2tog *, repeat from * to * 5 times, k1. (54sts)
Row 10: Purl.
Row 11: K6, k2tog, * k7, k2tog *, repeat from * to * 5 times, k1. (48sts)
Row 12: Purl.
Row 13: K1, k2tog across work to the last st, k1.
27sts remain.

♥ Cut your thread and then thread it through all the sts, pulling it tightly.

♥ Use this thread to sew the side seam as far as the opening for the spout, where the 2-st garter st edging finishes.

♥ Sew the bottom side seam to where the 2-st garter st edging begins.

♥ Work your motif (here, a tea cup; see pattern on page 240) using chain st (see page 225) and a contrasting colour of wool.

♥ Tack the shape first, if you like, working out from the centre of the tea cosy to ensure the motif is central. Work a running st (see page 226) box around the image in a contrasting colour of wool.

♥ Make a pompom (see page 152) and attach securely to the top.

Bring back the
patch!

DESIGNER CLOTHES ARE EXPENSIVE, and cheap-as-chips high-street items often fall apart after a single season. So it pays to make the clothes that we have and love last longer. These days it is also rather smart – it says you're not a shopaholic, that you care for the environment and have more on your mind than being seen with the latest must-have accessory. Posh people, particularly older ones, are famous for wearing their clothes until they literally fall apart. Care for your clothes by washing only when necessary, using gentle detergents, and protecting from house moths with lavender bags (see page 62), pomanders (see page 174) and pheromone traps. And should the worst come to the worst and a hole or worn patch appear, don't chuck it, mend it!

Patching clothes doesn't have to make you look like an extra from *The Waltons* – do it in style and you can wear your patches with pride. If you're handy with a needle, your patches can be objects of beauty. Rather than trying to match the main fabric, make a feature of the patch by using a contrasting colour, ideally in a luxurious texture, such as silk or velvet. Turn over the edges and iron and tack into position before machine or hand sewing with small neat stitches. If you want, you can even add a decorative top layer of stitching in a contrasting or eye-catching thread, such as black silk blanket stitch or silver or gold chain stitch (see page 225).

If sewing is not your thing, try hiding the offending hole with a pretty brooch or flower corsage (see page 150). Felt flowers, simply cut with scissors, layered in contrasting or coordinating colours and secured with a sequin or bead in the centre (see also page 146)are all the rage and can look as good on a cashmere jersey as they do on a pair of jeans. Think Sarah Jessica Parker and *Sex and the City* rather than *Blue Peter*. It's all a matter of attitude.

Button
power!

THE QUICKEST WAY to update a garment is to change the buttons – either with a matched set or, which can be more fun, an eclectic mix of old and new. This vintage jacket had three self-covered velvet buttons, but has been given a quirky contemporary makeover simply by substituting three different buttons all of the same size. The same idea, using a row of smaller buttons, also looks great on a cardigan.

Our mothers always had tins full of old and new buttons all awaiting their moment – a good stash of them makes a wonderful resource. (The contents of a button tin, with a cup cake or muffin tin for sorting the different sizes and colours, can also keep young children amused for hours – though do be aware of the potential danger of babies swallowing and choking on buttons.) Get into the habit of collecting attractive buttons, removing them from clothes that have become too worn to recycle, or picking up nice ones from haberdashery counters, junk shops and antiques fairs. It is sometimes worth buying the occasional item from a thrift shop or jumble sale simply for the buttons.

Try using your button stash in unusual ways – for instance, the backs of shell buttons are often more interesting than the fronts; or try adding extra buttons between the functioning ones, to make them more of a feature. Buttonholes can always be neatly enlarged to fit a slightly bigger button (see page 227, for how to stitch a buttonhole) or sewn a little smaller to ensure a snugger fit.

For other button ideas, see the Button light pull on page 168, Homemade cards on page 178 and Valentine's heart (worn here as a bracelet) on page 16.

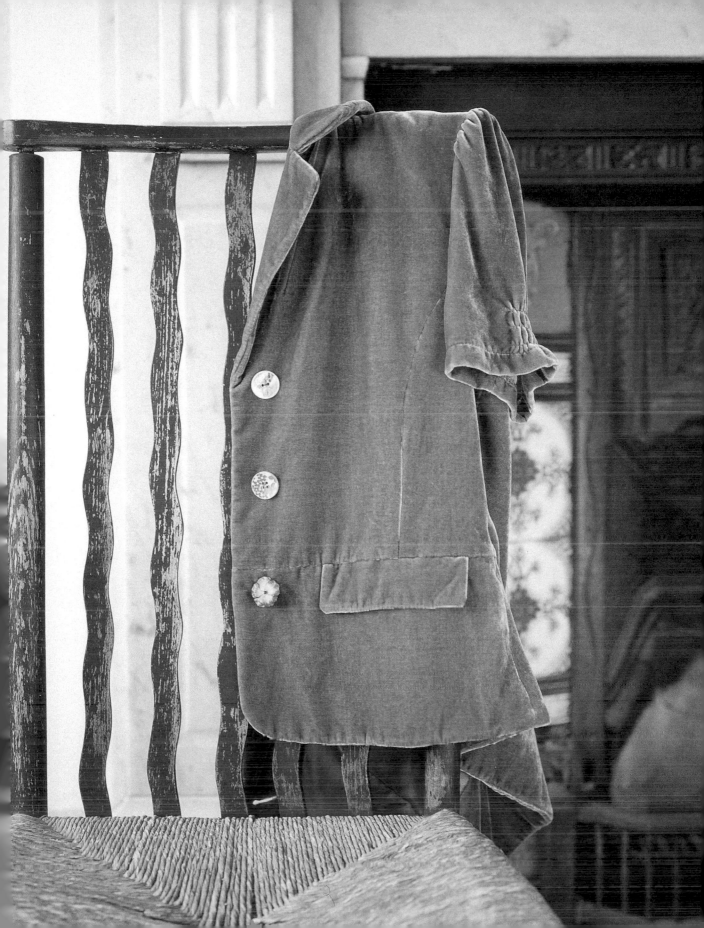

Our mothers always had tins full of old and new buttons all awaiting their moment – a good stash of them makes a wonderful resource.

Felt flower hair clips and
combs

THESE CHARMING FELT hair accessories are fun and fashionable, and also deceptively simple to make. Children old enough to safely manipulate a pair of sharp scissors should be able to make them with some parental supervision – and they make great presents or items to sell at a school fête.

Flower clip or comb

You will need

◆ Scraps of felt in contrasting colours
◆ Cotton thread in matching colours
◆ Hair clip
◆ Undecorated hair comb

To make

♥ Cut a strip of felt approximately 10cm (4in) by between 1.5 and 2.5cm (½ and 1in), depending on how big you want your flowers. Cut one edge with pinking shears, then with standard scissors cut between each 'v' of the pinked edge to approximately 5mm (¼in) from the opposite edge (see page 149).

♥ For the flower centre, cut a piece of felt in a contrasting colour 5cm x 5mm (2 x ¼in). Roll it up to form the centre of your flower and then roll the petal strip around it, sewing the edges and underside securely to hold it all together.

♥ For a simple hair clip, use just one or two flowers (see page 148); if making a comb slide, make five in various colours and sizes (see opposite). Then progress as follows.

♥ For the hair clip, cut a leaf shape in double-thickness felt and sew around the edge with running stitch, with a line down the centre to form the leaf vein (see overleaf). Sew the flower to one end of the leaf and then sew the leaf to a hair clip, securing it in three places by sewing over the straight edge of the clip and the underside of the leaf with a small over stitch.

♥ For the comb, cut a piece of felt the width of the comb by 2cm (¾in) or double the depth of the top of the comb. Stitch the felt around the top of the comb, sewing between each tooth and also sewing the ends together neatly. Sew the five flowers in a random order on to the felt edge of your comb, stitching from the underneath where it will not show. You can add narrow strips of felt looped over in between the flowers to add more texture or make some small leaves from green felt and sew neatly in place.

Flower corsage

FLORAL FABRIC CORSAGES are back in fashion, adding instant glamour to a party dress or perking up a plain shirt or sweater. This corsage is simple to make, and can be given endless variations by using different colours and textures of old and new fabrics. A group of them would look great on a belt or waistband – and they can even be used to hide the odd worn patch or moth hole on a much-loved cashmere jersey (see also Bring back the patch! on page 140). This design was inspired by a corsage seen at a textiles show several years ago and would be a fun project for a crafts club, where an attractive selection could be created in the course of an evening.

You will need

- ◆ Scraps of fabric in contrasting materials, colours and patterns
- ◆ Cotton thread for hand or machine sewing
- ◆ Brooch pin (optional)

To make

♥ Cut various size circles of fabrics and layer them five or six deep, using a variety of different thicknesses and textures, such as velvet and net. Use pinking shears for some to give added interest around the edge.

♥ Sew four lines across the diameter of the circles, forming eight segments (see above right), machine or hand sewing as you choose. You can always use silver thread, as shown here, and leave loose strands at the edges by not trimming too close – to add to the overall effect of this piece.

♥ Cut between each line of stitching to just short of the centre. Then turn over the corsage and pinch together each segment near the centre (below right), sewing each in place to give the flower a three-dimensional shape.

♥ Sew the finished corsage firmly into place; if you want to be able to transfer the corsage from garment to garment, attach a brooch pin to the back.

Pompoms

POMPOMS CAN BE used in all sorts of fun and stylish ways: apart from imparting a jaunty air to hats or berets, they can be added to anything from a tea cosy (see page 138) to a child's toy, or made up in festive colours as Christmas tree or birthday decorations. A cluster of three or five smaller pompoms can transform a child's beanie hat into something rather special, or be attached to cord or lengths of twisted wool to make attractive drawstrings for clothes or children's gloves.

You will need
♦ Cardboard
♦ Darning needle or bobbin
♦ Yarn

To make

♥ Cut two cardboard circles with the diameter of your required size of pompom. Cut out a smaller circle in the centre (to the proportions shown right).

♥ With the yarn threaded through a large darning needle or bobbin, wind it all around the doughnut shape, tightly and thickly.

♥ When the cardboard is covered and you can hardly get your needle through the central hole, cut the yarn all around the outer edge of the circle and secure by tying another piece of yarn tightly around the centre of the pompom.

♥ Remove the cardboard and fluff up the pompom. Trim with a pair of sharp scissors to even it up into a perfect ball. This can also help the edges of the yarn to fluff up nicely.

♥ Attach your pompom securely with matching yarn to whatever you are making.

Autumn chandelier

CREATING SIMPLE AUTUMNAL mobiles using colourful leaves, bright luscious berries and seedheads suspended from twiggy branches is a great way to make use of the items picked up on a walk in the park or countryside. This elegant autumn chandelier takes the idea one step further, and is only a little more complicated to make. We used scarlet Virginia creeper (*Parthenocissus quinquefolia*) with the fronds of the crimson glory vine (*Vitis coignetiae*) for the base and suspended it from strings of rosehips. Hanging from a tree branch or pergola, it looks especially beautiful when backlit by the low rays of the autumn sun, but could be hung indoors in a hallway for an autumn party. For an evening gathering, you can even wire in night-lights in holders or string night-lights in glass jars (see also page 92)from the underneath, but take care to leave gaps in the foliage directly above the flames and a good few inches on either side. (In any case, never leave naked candle flames unattended.) Or just enjoy it on your own, out in the garden on an Indian summer's evening, with a warm throw over your lap and a glass of sloe gin in your hand (see page 162).

You will need

♦ Ivy or straw
♦ Plenty of florist's wire
♦ Brightly coloured autumn foliage in reds, oranges and yellows
♦ 2 x 90cm (36in) lengths of string
♦ Darning needle
♦ Rosehips, or cranberries for a more Christmassy feel
♦ Night-lights in glass jars (optional)

To make

♥ Create the base of the chandelier by laying out the ivy leaves(or straw) to make a length of about 1m (1yd) and lashing together by wrapping round and round with the florist's wire. Join the two ends together into a wreath shape and bind together with more florist's wire.

♥ Make a leafy garland by attaching the different foliage and berries using more florist's wire. Work your way around the circular frame, checking for gaps and making sure it is balanced and pleasing to the eye. Individual leaves or small clusters of berries can be added at the end to fill any gaps.

♥ For each berry 'chain', thread one end of the string through the eye of the darning needle and thread together the rosehips or cranberries one by one, leaving approximately 10cm (4in) of string at either end. When both strings are complete, tie each end to the wreath to form two arcs of berries over the wreath; the point where they cross is where you hang the chandelier from.

♥ To illuminate for evenings, attach night-lights at four points around the chandelier. To do this, remove the wax candles, pierce two holes in the base of each metal case and attach with florist's wire to the chandelier. Each candle can then be replaced easily whenever the previous one burns out. Just be sure there is no foliage directly above the flame. Alternatively, hang night-lights in glass jars from the bottom of the wreath (see page 92) – these are less likely to blow out in the breeze – but again, make sure the flames are not directly below any foliage.

Spicy pumpkin soup

SERVED IN A PUMPKIN shell cauldron from which the flesh has been carved, this spicy aromatic soup is ideal festive fare for Hallowe'en and Bonfire Night parties. The cheapest way to acquire a large pumpkin like this is to grow your own – they are spectacularly easy to grow from seed in spring. Just give them a good fertile patch (the top or edge of a compost bay or pile is highly recommended by some people) and plenty of water and watch the fruits swell. For a touch of ghoulish mystery at Hallowe'en, put the lid on the pumpkin as you take it to the table and the steam will creep out through the holes.

You will need

- 1 x 2.5kg (5½lb) pumpkin (yields 600g (1lb 6oz) flesh)
- 2 tbsp olive oil
- 250g (9oz) onions, peeled and sliced
- 1 tsp mustard seeds
- 2 cloves garlic, peeled and crushed
- 1 tsp cinnamon
- 1 tsp cumin
- ½ tsp turmeric
- ½ tsp celery salt (optional)
- 250g (9oz) carrots, peeled and chopped
- 500ml (18fl oz) vegetable stock
- Salt and freshly ground black pepper
- 150ml (5fl oz) milk
- Single cream, to serve

To make

♥ Using a very sharp knife, carefully cut off the lid of the pumpkin about one-third of the way down. Scrape out the seeds and put in the compost or dry them to sow next spring to grow next year's pumpkins. Scrape out as much of the flesh as you can using a large metal spoon; scraping upwards is most effective. You should end up with about 600g (1lb 6oz) of flesh, depending on how close you scrape to the skin.

♥ In a large saucepan, heat the olive oil. Add the onions and sauté until clear. Then add the mustard seeds and garlic. Sauté for a further minute and add the remaining spices and celery salt (if using). Mix together and cook for a further minute. Remove from the heat and add the pumpkin, carrots and stock. Season to taste with salt and pepper.

♥ Return to the heat and bring to the boil. Then reduce the heat and simmer for 20 minutes or until the pumpkin and carrots are soft. Remove from heat and leave to cool slightly.

♥ Purée the soup in a food processor or with a hand-held blender. Add the milk and heat through gently.

♥ When ready to serve, pour the soup carefully into the empty pumpkin shell, add a swirl of single cream and serve with slices of toast rubbed with olive oil and garlic.

Golden autumn
chutney

IT'S ALWAYS GOOD to have a tasty chutney recipe handy for using up any gluts of fruit or vegetables from the garden – or for cooking up end-of-season bargains from the greengrocer or farmer's market. This all-purpose favourite was passed on from a friend's grandmother who always seemed to be stirring a steaming vat of jam or chutney in early autumn. It has the advantage of being flexible – just vary the main ingredients depending on what you have available. The turmeric gives a lovely golden colour, and adding some of the chopped pieces of fruit or vegetable a little later in the cooking makes for a bit of texture – a welcome relief from the dark brown sludge that all too often gives chutney a bad name.

You will need

◆ 6 cooking or eating apples, peeled, cored and finely chopped
◆ 1.35kg (3lb) assorted vegetables including courgettes, green beans and green tomatoes, chopped up small
◆ 6 onions, peeled and diced
◆ 1 red chilli pepper, deseeded and finely chopped
◆ 2 tbsp peeled and finely grated or chopped root ginger
◆ 1 stick of cinnamon
◆ 2 tbsp honey or demerara sugar
◆ 1 tsp allspice
◆ 1 tsp ground cloves
◆ 1 tbsp turmeric
◆ 1 tsp coarse salt
◆ 1 litre (1¾ pints) cider vinegar
◆ 6 x 450g (1lb) sterilized jars (see page 233)

To make

♥ Divide the chopped apples and vegetables into three equal piles. Place two-thirds in a large saucepan or jam-making cauldron with all of the other ingredients and bring to the boil.

♥ Simmer for 50 minutes before adding the remaining chopped pieces for a final 10 minutes. Remove the cinnamon stick and pour the chutney, using a funnel, into the sterilized glass jars. Close the lids tightly and label.

Sloe gin

BLACK WITH A GRAPE-LIKE BLOOM, sloes can be found in abundance in country hedgerows in autumn. Though bitter to eat, they impart a delicious flavour and jewel-like colour to gin when steeped for several months. Treat damsons and blackberries in the same way – and you can always use vodka instead of gin, adding a vanilla pod for extra sweetness. Picking sloes and damsons is more fun if you take an old-fashioned walking stick for gently pulling down the higher branches, where the best fruit is often lurking, just out of reach. The following recipe makes enough for two standard-sized bottles (70cl), which can then be divided between several smaller bottles.

You will need

♦ About 450g (1lb) sloes, damsons or blackberries, well washed
♦ Sugar to taste – most recipes suggest one-third fruit to one-third alcohol to one-third sugar, but this can be too sweet for some
♦ 70cl bottle of cheap gin or vodka
♦ Cinnamon sticks (optional)
♦ Juniper berries (optional)
♦ Almond essence with damsons; vanilla pod with blackberries (optional)
♦ Muslin cloth
♦ Sterilized bottles (see page 233)

To make

♥ Put the washed fruit into plastic bags and place in the freezer for a week, where the cold will break down the skins. This is much easier than the traditional method of pricking the fruit all over.

♥ Fill two bottles or large jars nearly half way (three-eighths) with fruit, add another eighth of sugar to bring it up to half way and then fill to the top with gin. Add a couple of cinnamon sticks or a few juniper berries for extra flavour if you want, and a few drops of almond essence with the damsons or a vanilla pod to the blackberries.

♥ Place the jars where you will remember to shake or swirl the fruit around every other day for a total of two months. When it is ready to bottle, pass the liquid through a doubled piece of muslin several times to clarify.

♥ Discard the sloes – though the soused damsons are good with ice cream – and, then, using a funnel, pour into pretty glass bottles you've been saving, and label. The gin is ready to drink after three months, but is best left for a year.

Quince
brandy

IF YOU HAVE a quince tree in your garden, you'll be familiar with that guilty feeling every autumn when, lost in wonder at the sight of their golden beauty, you also don't know *quite* what to do with the piles of fruit gathering on the grass or in bowls and bags around your kitchen. Quince jelly, or *membrillo*, while delicious, is terribly time-consuming to make, involving lots of boiling and straining through muslin. In contrast, this quince brandy is simplicity itself – you don't even have to core and peel the fruit. It can be drunk on its own, added to cocktails or used to soak dried fruit for fruit cakes or mince pies. In pretty, clear glass jars or bottles, with a ribbon or handwritten label around the neck, it also makes a lovely present. The amount below fills one 5-litre (8¾-pint) jar or several smaller containers.

You will need
- 4–6 quinces
- 4 bottles cheap brandy
- 3–4 cinnamon sticks
- 6 star anise
- Sterlized bottles or large jar (see page 233)

To make
♥ Wipe the quinces clean and cut them into quarters or large chunks without peeling or coring. Place the fruit in a large clear glass jar and pour the brandy over to cover the fruit and fill to the top.

♥ With a long-handled spoon, carefully push in the cinnamon sticks and star anise so they can be seen from around the edges, and seal with the lid. Leave for at least six weeks before drinking – the longer the better.

winter

Button light
pull

USING AN ATTRACTIVE PEBBLE or favourite button is a great way to add individuality to a boring old light pull. But why stop at just one? Buttons of all shapes, sizes and colours have been threaded together here to make this stylishly sculptural pull, which feels as good as it looks. You may well already have a button tin packed full of treasures (see page 142). This project is good for using up those buttons that never seem to get chosen over the years, or ones that have been taken off an item of clothing in order to update it with different buttons (see also page 142). For a different look, why not restrict yourself to one or two colours – just white and/or mother-of-pearl would look stunning – to coordinate with the colours you have used to decorate the rest of the room? The same method could also be used for an interior bell pull – inside a porch, for instance.

You will need
- Strong string (use string rather than cord, as some of the holes in the button may be small)
- Collection of buttons
- Sticky tape

To make
♥ Tie a knot at the bottom of the string, winding the thread around two holes in the bottom button for extra security.

♥ Start threading your buttons, varying the mix all the way up, even adding one or two buttons with sideways (shank-back) holes for a quirky touch. Wrapping sticky tape around the end of the string will prevent it fraying.

♥ Stop where you feel the pull looks good – or when your supply of buttons runs out! You can go right up to the ceiling if you want. Secure the top button with a knot and cut the string, leaving a little spare for tying.

♥ To finish, stand on a chair or stepladder and tie your button pull securely to the cord pull already hanging from the ceiling, trimming the ends neatly.

Victorian
sand pincushion

HERE IS A contemporary spin on a technique that was popular in Victorian times. Pincushions such as this one, decorated with pins pushed in to create elaborate dedications and designs, were made to commemorate births, weddings and other occasions and were often given as presents. Here, the idea has been revived, but brought up to date by simplifying the design and using a fashionable dark purple velvet for the background. Using sand from a garden centre or hardware store to stuff the cushion makes it heavy enough to be used as a bookend or paperweight. And pushing pins through the fabric into the sand is strangely satisfying and absorbing. Using diamante-style pins is a nice touch.

You will need

- Scraps of plain velvet or similar fabric
- Cotton thread for machine sewing
- 1.2kg (2½lb) sand for a cushion measuring 18 x 16cm (7 x 6¼in)
- Tissue paper (optional)
- 1 pack of dressmaker's or diamante-style pins

To make

♥ Cut out two pieces of fabric each measuring approximately 18 x 16cm (7 x 6¼in). Place together, right sides together, and machine sew around the edges with very small stitches so the sand cannot find a way out, leaving a small gap on one edge. To be sure that you avoid sand leaking out, you could always make an inner bag in calico or fine cotton. Trim the corner seams, turn right sides out, iron into shape and fill tightly with sand. Sew up the opening neatly.

♥ Decide on your design. Work freehand from a drawing or sketch it out on tissue paper, pinning the paper in place and working your design through it on to the cushion and then tearing the paper away afterwards.

♥ Begin sticking in your pins to create the design, working methodically from the middle out, to ensure symmetry.

♥ Be sure to keep the pincushion well away from small children, to whom the pins could be harmful.

Hot-water bottle cover

THIS COSY HOT-WATER bottle cover is not only a clever way to make use of an old or felted jersey; it's also an improvement on many similar covers that are sold in the shops. By making the opening at the bottom, rather than at the top end of the cover, the danger of damage when stretching it over the stopper end of the bottle is reduced. You can make it from an old blanket or similar thick fabric, but the stretch in the knitting makes an old jersey ideal – it's a great use for one that has holes in elsewhere, or has been felted by washing at too hot a temperature. Felted wool or even cashmere has a lovely texture and is great for this purpose as it won't unravel. Choose one with an attractive edging if possible, taking care when you lay it out to make the natural edge of the jersey the edge of the 'flap' in the cover.

You will need

◆ Large piece of paper
◆ Old jersey
◆ Cotton thread to match

To make

♥ Draw around your hot-water bottle, adding 1.5cm (½in) all around for a seam allowance. Then make two paper pattern pieces as follows:

PIECE A must be at least 5cm (2in) longer than Piece B and incorporate the natural edge of the jersey at the bottom. PIECE B needs to be approximately 1cm (½in) shorter than the hot-water bottle.

Cutting the pattern pieces to these dimensions allows for the longer piece (A) to overlap the base of the bottle and also the shorter piece, thus creating the envelope opening.

♥ Cut out the two pattern pieces from your fabric, being sure to place the bottom edge of each pattern piece along the natural edge of the knitting.

♥ Fold up the bottom 5cm (2in) of Piece A, right side to right side, and pin or tack in place at the edges. Then, with right sides facing, place together the two pieces, matching up the tops. Piece B should be about 1cm (½in) shorter than Piece A.

♥ Sew around the cover using a small zigzag stitch on a sewing machine or use back stitch (see page 225) if sewing by hand. Do not sew along the folded edge.

♥ Turn right sides out and bring the 5cm (2in) fold to the front to create the envelope edge that secures your hot-water bottle in place.

Citrus
pomander

MADE AND USED since Elizabethan times, a pomander is a natural air-freshener and moth repellant that is just as effective today. Tuck some in your clothes drawers and laundry cupboards, hang from wardrobe rails or stack several in a bowl instead of potpourri. Oranges are most commonly used, but lemons or limes work just as well, their strong aroma mingling with that of the spices. Pomanders take patience to make, but can be an enjoyable project for children – and make lovely Mothering Sunday presents. They last for many years; if the scent is fading, add a few drops of clove oil to the spice mix and roll the pomanders in it again.

You will need (per pomander)

- Small or medium-sized unblemished citrus fruit
- Masking tape or 2 elastic bands
- 25g (1oz) large-headed cloves
- Fine knitting needle, skewer or cocktail stick
- Paper bag to fit fruit
- 1 tsp each of cinnamon, nutmeg and ground cloves or a tablespoon of ready-made mixed spice
- 1 tsp ground orris root (available from healthfood shops – can be omitted, but helps preserve the pomander)
- Ribbon for hanging
- Dressmaker's pin or PVA glue

To make

♥ Take your fruit and, using masking tape or elastic bands, mark out the space on the fruit where the ribbon will lie. This makes it easier to wrap the ribbon around the pomander once it has dried.

♥ Stick the whole cloves into the fruit, beginning at the navel and working a line all around the fruit, then a parallel line around your ribbon space, keeping to a symmetrical pattern where possible. If the skin seems tough, make holes first using a knitting needle, skewer or cocktail stick. The cloves need to be fairly close together but not quite touching.

♥ Mix together the ground spices and orris root, if using, on a plate and when the fruit is covered with cloves, roll it in the powder. Place in a paper bag and leave in a dry, dark place for 6–8 weeks. (Do not use a plastic bag as it will prevent the pomander from drying.)

♥ During the drying process, the clove oil should preserve the orange skin, but if you notice any mould or decomposition, throw it out and start again. The pomander is fully dry when it has shrunk and sounds light and hollow when tapped. Shake off any excess spices.

♥ Wrap the ribbon around the fruit, securing with a dressmaker's pin or PVA glue at the base, and make a loop or bow at the top for hanging.

Homemade
cards

MAKING YOUR OWN greetings cards is satisfying on many different levels. It saves money and provides a useful and enjoyable wet-weather activity. It also means that you always have a stash of gorgeous one-off cards to send to friends or relations, whatever the occasion – handmade cards are always appreciated and are usually kept for far longer than ready-made ones.

When it comes to designs, they can be as simple or complex as your time and abilities allow. The very simplest ideas can be wonderfully effective: for instance, the card shown here was created by sticking just one heart-shaped pressed leaf on to card and writing a short message by hand. This was a morning glory leaf that had just started to turn a deep shade of autumnal copper, picked and pressed between sheets of paper in a large heavy book, with other books left on top to weight it down for a couple of weeks. (If you have an Aga or Rayburn, a good way of pressing leaves is to sandwich them between the sheets of an entire newspaper section and place them beneath rugs in front of the Aga where passing feet will walk over them.)

The other ideas illustrated involve a little sewing – collages of buttons and simple running stitches worked on to coloured felt. Cutting out the shapes with pinking shears adds to the decorative effect, and a similar-sized piece can be glued on to the inside front of the card to hide knots and so on. Sewn cards take a little longer, but can be done quite easily while watching television or listening to the radio. Other ideas include recycling old unused photographs of flowers, children and so on, or snipping around and mounting children's drawings.

Handmade cards are always appreciated and are usually kept for far longer than ready-made ones.

with love ♡

Crochet squares

LIKE KNITTING, crochet has lost its former fuddy-duddy image to become highly fashionable, with designers such as Dolce & Gabbana and Vivienne Westwood sending crocheted dresses and accessories down the catwalks in recent years. Luckily, it is even easier than knitting to learn, and can become quite addictive! Crochet squares, joined together in a funky-coloured patchwork, are a perennial favourite – and are also the simplest and easiest way to start. Once you have mastered the basic square, several can be joined together to make anything from a simple scarf or cushion cover to a large double blanket like this one.

Traditionally a way of using up scraps of leftover yarn, patchwork crochet has to be carefully planned if it is not to end up looking a disordered mess. This blanket, bought in a thrift shop, was made in the 1940s by someone who clearly had a keen sense of colour and design. Though each square is random in colour and order for the first three rounds (rings of crocheting, starting in the middle of the square, see page 183), it is coordinated with the surrounding squares for the final, outer round – a brown marl for the squares that make up the central panel, then apple green, and finishing with blue for the wide surround that hangs down the bed. This simple discipline really draws the design together – if you look carefully you can see squares using the same or similar colours distributed irregularly but reasonably evenly throughout the blanket. A similar effect could be achieved by working out which yarn you have most of and using it to work the outer round of each of your squares. Turn the page for instructions to start making your very own family heirloom.

You will need

◆ Yarns in assorted colours, but always the same weight (we have used doubleknitting (DK) yarn)

◆ 3.25mm crochet hook if using DK yarn

Abbreviations

See page 231

To make a single square

This is an easy, basic square for anyone who can crochet. For a good introduction to basic crochet skills, see the books and courses listed in the Directory on pages 245–6. The following makes a square measuring approximately 7.5cm (3in). Work each round in a different-colour yarn.

♥ With 3.25mm crochet hook and yarn, make 6ch. Join in a circle with a sl st.

ROUND 1: 5ch (count as 1tr and 2ch), 11tr into centre, sl st to 3rd of 5ch.

ROUND 2: Sl st into next ch, 5ch (count as 1tr and 3ch), 3tr into same space, * 1ch, miss 3tr (3tr, 2ch, 3tr) into next sp, repeat from * twice, 1ch, miss 3sts, 2tr into same sp as 5ch at beginning of round, sl st to 3rd of 5ch.

ROUND 3: Sl st into next ch, 5ch (count as 1tr and 2ch), 3tr into same sp, * 1ch, miss 3tr, 3tr into next sp, 1ch, miss 3tr **, (3tr, 2ch, 3tr) into next sp, rep from * twice, and from * to ** again, 2tr into same sp as 5ch, sl st to 3rd of 5ch.

ROUND 4: Sl st into next ch, 5ch (count as 1tr and 2ch), 3tr into same space, * (1ch, miss 3tr, 3tr into next sp) twice, 1ch, miss 3tr **, (3tr, 2ch, 3tr) into next sp, rep from * twice, and from * to ** again, 2tr into same sp as 5ch, sl st to 3rd of 5ch. Fasten off.

To sew together squares to make up a blanket

♥ Work as many squares as possible, thinking about your palette as discussed above. Join your squares together with dc by placing squares wrong sides together. Join all squares with the same colour throughout the blanket, keeping some aside for repairs.

♥ When the all the squares are joined together, work a border around the edge in the following way:

ROUND 1: Work 3tr 1ch into each space between 3trs of each square edge.

ROUNDS 2 TO 4: Work 1dc into each tr all around blanket. Fasten off.

The border can be worked in a plain colour or in different colours for each round, depending on the effect you want and how much yarn you have left.

Cross-stitch
no entry sign

CROSS STITCHING IS PERFECT for long winter evenings, when you want a restful yet creative task. Once you have mastered the basic technique, it can be done while watching an old film on television or talking to a friend. Many habitual cross-stitchers swear by its relaxing, almost meditative qualities: the mind is freed from outside worries but needs to stay present to the task to follow the pattern. Cross stitch is often associated with old-fashioned samplers, and you can easily make your own versions to dedicate a birth or marriage with a design incorporating names and dates and so on.

But why not give cross stitch a contemporary twist? Hand stitching is very much in fashion these days, with designers from Paul Smith to Marni and Dolce & Gabbana incorporating embroidery in their clothes. Instead of traditional designs using flowers, cats and animals, find inspiration in the artist Tracey Emin's take on needlework (you can see her travel bag on display in the fashion galleries at the V&A Museum in London) and think subversive. There can be charm and humour in the juxtaposition of the painstaking, timeworn techniques and an offbeat, unexpected message: 'GO AWAY' on a teenager's door, for instance, or 'LEAVE ME ALONE'. Here, a simple 'no entry' road sign has been fashioned in red thread on a white ground: you could add the words, too.

The internet is full of cross-stitch designs that can easily be copied and transferred to fabric (see page 225 for more information on cross stitch and the Directory, pages 243–4, for specialist suppliers).

Striped woolly
scarf

A LONG STRIPY SCARF makes a great addition to any outfit once the weather gets colder. This is just about the most simple scarf ever – perfect for novice knitters and suitable to be worn by men as well as women, of any age. The design uses basic garter stitch throughout, and incorporates lots of changes of colour, which, if done neatly, can look good on the reverse side, too. This is a great way to use up scraps of wool – just check that they are all of the same weight. Even very short lengths in contrasting colours can be used for the cast-on and cast-off edge, adding an attractive finish. Improvise and make up your own pattern, or stick to the simple instructions below.

You will need

- 200g (7oz) chunky yarn in main colour (duck egg) (MC)
- Approximately 30g (1¼oz) chunky yarn in colour B (orange) (col B)
- Approximately 30g (1¼oz) chunky yarn in colour C (green) (col C)
- 6.5mm (UK size 3; US size 10½) knitting needles

Abbreviations

See page 229

Tension over garter stitch

The yarn we used worked out at the following tension, but note the needle size and tension on your ball of wool (usually written on the ball band) in case it is different, and change accordingly.

14sts and 26 rows = 10cm (4in)

Measurements

22 x 115cm (8½ x 45in)

To make

♥ With 6.5mm needles (UK size 3; US size 10½) and col B, cast on 30sts.
Rows 1–4: Change to col C, knit.
Rows 5 & 6: Col B, knit.
Rows 7 & 8: MC, knit.
Rows 9 & 10: Col C, knit.
Rows 11 & 12: MC, knit.
Rows 13–16: Col B, knit.
Rows 17 & 18: Col C, knit.
Rows 19–22: MC, knit.
Rows 23 & 24: Col B, knit.
Rows 25 & 26: Col C, knit.
Rows 27–44: MC, knit.
Rows 45 & 46: Col B, knit.
Rows 47–52: MC, knit.
Rows 53 & 54: Col C, knit.
Rows 55–206: MC, knit.
Rows 207 & 208: Col C, knit.
Rows 209–214: MC, knit.
Rows 215 & 216: Col B, knit.
Rows 217–234: MC, knit.
Rows 235 & 236: Col C, knit.

Row 237–238: Col B, knit.
Rows 239–242: MC, knit.
Rows 243 & 244: Col C, knit.
Rows 245–248: Col B, knit.
Rows 249 & 250: MC, knit.
Rows 251 & 252: Col C, knit.
Rows 253 & 254: MC, knit.
Rows 255 & 256: Col B, knit.
Rows 257–260: Col C, knit.
Change to col B and cast off.
Weave in any loose ends.

♥ For a longer or shorter scarf, add or reduce rows between rows 55 and 206.

Fingerless gloves

THESE STRIPY GLOVES are warm and stylish while still leaving your fingers free. The pattern is ideal for using up ends of 4-ply wool – the pair of finished gloves weigh approximately 50g (2oz). It would be very easy to knit rainbow stripes from this pattern if you have a range of colours to hand. The gloves could also be knitted shorter by reducing the number of rows between rows 33 and 47, or made longer by knitting extra rows before the decreasing starts.

You will need

- 50g (2oz) of 4-ply wool in mixed colours (here we have used brown, aubergine and moss)
- 3.25mm (UK size 10; US size 3) knitting needles

Key

Colour A: brown (col A)
Colour B: aubergine (col B)
Colour C: moss (col C)

Abbreviations

See page 229

Tension

14sts and 18 rows = 5cm (2in)

Measurements

Finished length is approximately 26cm (10¼in)

These stripy gloves are warm and stylish while still leaving your fingers free...

To make the right glove

♥ With 3.25mm (UK size 10; US size 3) needles and col B, cast on 59sts.

Change to col A and work 6 rows in k1, p1 rib.

Dec 1st at end of row 6. (58sts) (NB For decreasing, knit together the 3rd and 4th sts from the edge. This produces a fashioning mark on the gloves, which gives them a more stylish finish.)

Cont with col A.

Row 1 (RS): Knit.

Row 2: Purl.

Row 3: Using col B, knit.

Row 4: Purl.

Row 5: Using col C, knit.

Row 6: Purl.

These 6 rows form the pattern.

Cont in pattern for stripes, dec 1st at each end of the following row and then on rows 15, 21, 27 and 33, until 48sts remain.

Cont until the beginning of row 47, then work thumb gusset as follows, keeping stripes correct.

Row 1 (RS): K24, inc in next st, k2, inc in next st, k20. (50sts)

Work 3 rows.

Row 5: K24, inc in next st, k4, inc in next st, k20. (52sts)

Work 3 rows.

Row 9: K24, inc in next st, k6, inc in next st, k20. (54sts)

Work 3 rows.

Row 13: K24, inc in next st, k8, inc in next st, k20. (56sts)

Work 3 rows.

Row 17: K24, inc in next st, k10, inc in next st, k20. (58sts)

Work 1 row.

Row 19: K38, turn and cast on 1st.

Row 20*: p14, turn and cast on 1st. (15sts)

Work 6 rows on these 15sts, keeping stripes correct.

Change to col A and work 2 rows in k1, p1 rib.

Cast off with col B.

Join the thumb seam.

With right sides facing, rejoin yarn, pick up 4sts from the thumb base (2 either side of seam) and cont to end of row.

Work 16 rows more.

Change to col A and work 4 rows in k1, p1 rib.

Change to col B and cast off.

To make the left glove

♥ Work as right to the beginning of thumb gusset shaping. Then work as follows:

Row 1 (RS): K19, inc in next st, k2, inc in next st, k25. (50sts)

Work 3 rows.

Row 5: K19, inc in next st, k4, inc in next st, k25. (52sts)

Work 3 rows.

Row 9: K19, inc in next st, k6, inc in next st, k25. (54sts)

Work 3 rows.

Row 13: K19, inc in next st, k8, inc in next st, k25. (56sts)

Work 3 rows.

Row 17: K19, inc in next st, k10, inc in next st, k25. (58sts)

Work 1 row.

Row 19: K33, turn and cast on 1st, cont as for right glove from *.

Making up

♥ Sew the side seam with mattress stitch (see website recommended on page 228), catching in ends where you can. Then sew in any remaining ends and press lightly with your iron on the wool setting.

Paperwhites on
pebbles

Forget expensive imported cut flowers in winter and fill your house with the fragrance of 'Paperwhite' narcissi from November until February. They look especially lovely at Christmas, when the pure-white star-like flowers provide a soothing contrast to the visual cacophony all around – and also make a wonderful present. The bulbs contain all they need to grow, so don't require soil. The flowers take five or six weeks to appear, so to ensure a good a Christmas show, plant them in late October. Each lot of flowers will last for a good few weeks, so for a continuous supply, prepare successive batches.

You will need

◆ Glass bowl or dish
◆ Pebbles, stone chippings or similar
◆ 'Paperwhite' narcissi bulbs (see Directory, page 247)
◆ Stick of artist's charcoal
◆ Water
◆ Ribbon or sticks, for support

To make

♥ Half fill the container with pebbles and arrange the bulbs carefully on top – you can cram 20 or more into a large dish for a stunning centrepiece, but just three or four in a smaller bowl will look great as well.

♥ Fill with water just to the base of the bulbs (they rot if fully immersed) and add a stick of artist's charcoal to the water to stop it stagnating and therefore smelling.

♥ Keep the container in a warm room and sit back and watch as snaky white roots anchor themselves around the stones, and green shoots sprout with buds concealed within.

♥ Flowering should start in five or six weeks – for a continuous supply have several containers on the go, starting a new one every two weeks.

♥ If the stems shoot up too high and become unruly, as often happens, bind the stems with pretty recycled ribbon, or add twiggy sticks or branches of catkins as supports.

♥ Presented in this way, with lots of buds yet to open, 'Paperwhites' make lovely Christmas presents – or give them in 'kit form' with all the components packed in a box with handwritten planting instructions.

Indoor
hyacinths

As FRAGRANT AS they are beautiful, hyacinths are the perfect indoor bulb for winter. Grown in containers or special 'forcing' jars, they also make lovely presents. Unlike most other plants, hyacinths can be grown successfully in pots without drainage holes, enabling you to press anything into use, from old painted mugs to small enamel buckets or vintage soup tureens. Or for presents, pot them up into pretty mugs or salad bowls that can later be washed out and used for their original purpose. Clear glass forcing jars are available from garden mail-order supplies (see Directory, page 248), but the most desirable ones, often in jewel-bright colours, date back to the 1950s and can sometimes be found in antique or junk shops.

To raise your own plants from bulbs, order or buy 'prepared' bulbs – which have been bred for early flowering – in late summer. Hyacinths need to be kept for 10–14 weeks in darkness to develop a strong root system and for the buds to appear, so for blooms at Christmas, start by mid-September. White is always a safe and stylish choice, but there are some good dark blues and purples around, such as the amethyst-coloured 'Woodstock' pictured here.

You will need
- 'Prepared' hyacinth bulbs (see above)
- Multi-purpose compost and florist's moss and container, or forcing jar
- Stick of artist's charcoal

To make
♥ If planting in soil, place the bulbs on a bed of damp compost and cover with more compost. Then cover with a layer of florist's moss, leaving only the very tops of the bulbs exposed.

♥ If using a forcing jar, fill the jar with water until the base of the bulb is no closer than a 5mm (¼in) away from the surface. The mere presence of water is enough to get the roots growing; bulbs rot if left to sit in water.

♥ Add a stick of artist's charcoal to the soil or water to prevent it stagnating and therefore smelling.

♥ Leave in the dark until the bud is clearly visible between the emerging leaves, checking to ensure the compost never dries out. Flowers should follow in a few weeks.

♥ Alternatively, buy cheap pots or trays of hyacinths in full bud and pot up as above, rinsing the roots carefully if you are using forcing jars.

Christmas
wreath

THIS NATURALLY BEAUTIFUL festive wreath is a far cry from the tinselly, trussed-up versions available in shops and markets, which are often so heavy on dark gloomy greenery. It is also surprisingly fun and easy to make, and will be much admired on your front door for a good two to three weeks. For the cheapest, greenest and most natural effect, you would ideally forage your own foliage from garden or hedgerow – ivy in particular needs a good annual prune, so you'd be doing it a favour. Or you can buy it all in – it's worth making an early-morning trip to a flower market and buying enough to supply a few like-minded friends, too. Why not get a few wreath-makers together for an informal workshop in your house? Fuelled by a simple yet delicious supper and a glass or two of mulled wine, much fun will be had and the wreaths will grow, like patchwork quilts, while you chat and work.

You will need
- Whippy willow branches
- Trailing ivy
- Roll of florist's wire
- Holly leaves
- Holly or other red berries
- Fir cones
- Mossy twigs
- Hydrangea head – the redder the better
- Strong ribbon or string for hanging

To make

🤍 Lay out the whippy willow branches to the desired circumference for your wreath. Lay long strands of ivy on top of it and lash all layers tightly together with the florist's wire to make a long sausage of foliage. This gives your wreath a good solid base and will help keep a strong round shape. (It's possible just to use holly and ivy as a base, but you may find that the weight of larger wreaths will cause them to stretch into an oval when hanging.)

🤍 Form the sausage into a wreath shape and secure the ends together with wire. This makes the base of the wreath.

🤍 Then, working around the wreath, attach holly leaves, berries, cones, twigs and sections from the hydrangea head, and any other Christmassy foliage, evenly around the circumference, securing each with the florist's wire.

🤍 When you have gone round once, hang the wreath to view from a distance, and continue to add more leaves and berries if any part looks sparse.

🤍 Attach a length of strong ribbon or string at the top back of the wreath where it will not show, for tying around a nail or hook on your door.

🤍 The wreath should last a good three weeks if hanging outside and may even dry out sufficiently to carry on as an indoor decoration, to be supplemented with seasonal flowers and foliage, throughout the rest of the year.

Advent
calendar

MADE FROM AN old linen sheet with 24 hand-painted pockets, this beautiful advent calendar is a cut above the disposable commercial ones available in the shops. Reusable year after year, it has the scope to become a family heirloom handed down through the generations. This is a project a whole family or school class could work on together – each person choosing a number of pockets to decorate. Or, if you want a more uniform look, you could do as we did and ask a talented friend (in our case the artist Mary Mathieson) to paint the entire design. The joy of it is that you can put whatever you like in the pockets: chocolates are by no means out of bounds (we used them here), or you could use small toys, pieces of a nativity scene that then get built up elsewhere, or other treasures. The pattern below uses a sewing machine but the project could be done by hand.

You will need

- An old sheet, or plain linen or cotton at least 82 x 125cm (32 x 50in) or 1.25m (50in) of 90cm (36in) wide fabric if buying specially
- Fabric paints and fabric crayons
- Assorted cotton threads for machine sewing
- Piece of dowelling approximately 76cm (30in)
- Ribbon for hanging

To make

♥ From the fabric, cut a piece measuring 74 x 82cm (29 x 32in). Then cut out 23 smaller pieces of various sizes for the pockets.

Six pieces each of the following sizes:

11 x 11cm (4½ x 4½in)
11 x 13cm (4½ x 5in)
12 x 12cm (4¾ x 4¾in)

Five pieces measuring:

13 x 15cm (5 x 6in)

Then, finally, one piece measuring:

15 x 15cm (6 x 6in) for the central Christmas Eve pocket.

♥ Using the fabric paints and fabric crayons, decorate each piece with a number from 1 to 23 and other Christmas images, if you like, perhaps using favourite cards or images from the internet for inspiration. Decorate the 15 x 15cm (6 x 6in) piece with a special image for Christmas Eve – we painted an angel.

♥ Make sure to leave at least 1cm (½in) around the image on all sides for hemming and attaching to the background.

♥ When all the small pieces are decorated, fold over 1cm (½in) along the top of each one, press and then hem with a contrasting-coloured thread. We chose a stitch on the sewing machine from the embroidery settings (nothing complicated as the sewing machine is 40 years old), but it looks very effective (see above). You might find other possibilities.

♥ Carefully fold in the three other sides on each piece by 1cm (½in) and iron to hold (see opposite). They are then all ready to attach to the background piece.

♥ Pin each pocket randomly on to the large piece, mixing up the numbers. Then sew around the three folded sides of each pocket to secure, using a standard machine running stitch.

♥ When all 24 pockets are attached, fold over 1cm (½in) all around the main piece and iron to hold. Then fold over another 1cm (½in) on the two side and bottom edges. Sew around these three sides with the same stitch and coloured thread used to hem the pocket tops.

♥ To make the channel at the top for hanging, fold over the top edge by 2cm (¾in) and sew across. Thread the dowelling through the channel, attach the ribbon to either end and hang in position ready to fill with goodies for the days leading up to Christmas Eve. We used chocolate coins and chocolate tree decorations.

Wrapping presents

In Britain alone, 8,000 tonnes of wrapping paper is used every year just on Christmas presents – the equivalent of 50,000 trees. It's un-ecological, uneconomical and, in many cases, not even very attractive. Why buy into the wasteful gift-wrap industry when you can easily make or recycle your own? Get into the habit of keeping and recycling wrapping paper and save ribbons from clothes purchases or bunches of flowers as well as from other presents. Set aside a drawer or large box to store it in – the paper neatly folded and the ribbons carefully rolled – and keep scissors, sticky tape, silver pens and other handy items there, too.

With the best will in the world, you will probably have to buy *some* paper. Tissue paper is cheap, recyclable and easy to work with – and comes in jewel-bright colours. Layer two colours for an interesting mix, and choose a coordinating ribbon. Brown paper is a timeless classic, and easily smartened up with a band of contrasting-patterned paper from your recycled stash. Even black and white newspaper can look beautiful if teamed with bright red or silver ribbon, and is great for large, unwieldy gifts. Or go for a roll of white drawing paper, hand painting or potato printing designs of your choice (see page 28 for tips) or spelling the recipient's name in bright colours (children are great at this and can be cajoled or bribed into doing batches at a time). For small presents, use wallpaper samples, or photocopy textured fabric, such as a piece of crochet, on plain paper.

The key when saving on paper is to wrap the presents beautifully, as here. Place awkwardly shaped items in boxes first, and fold the paper carefully round the gift, using 'hospital corners' as if making a bed (pulling the paper out straight from each end of the package and then folding in the edges diagonally to form a triangle). And let rip with the other adornments – use really good ribbon (cheap as chips when it is recycled), or glue on pompoms (see page 152) or lots of brightly coloured shapes, sequins or other decorative items from children's crafts kits. Layer one or two bands of ornate recycled paper around the present and tuck in a fresh or dried flower from the garden.

Many of the above ideas are illustrated opposite – for more on homemade cards see page 178.

Knitted
angel

THE ANGEL AT THE TOP is traditionally the finishing touch for any Christmas tree – the final task in the annual ritual of decorating the branches (see Felt decorations on page 215). And what could be prettier than this little knitted angel? She may look fiddly but, in fact, is easy enough for anyone with a basic mastery of knit and purl stitches; the only relatively time-consuming part would be the shaping on the wings and head. A nice idea would be to make a few as Christmas presents for friends and family – then practice can make perfect! The pattern below can also be adapted to make little dolls for children; just leave out the wings and change the colours of the dress. The hair is simplicity itself as it is made from loops of running stitch with the wool not pulled tight. It goes without saying that small items such as this are great for using up any scraps or lengths of wool you might have left over from other creative projects.

You will need
♦ 4-ply wool in the following colours (use up ends to make this angel as it takes tiny amounts): 10g (½oz) cream, tan or skin tone, pink, yellow or something for hair
♦ 3.25mm (UK size 10; US size 12) knitting needles
♦ Stuffing or cotton wool

Tension over stocking stitch
14sts and 18 rows = 5cm (2in)

Abbreviations
See page 229

Arms (make 2)
Cast on 10sts in cream, 2sts in tan.
Work 6 rows in stocking st (knit one row, purl one row).
Cast off 12sts.
The arms and legs naturally roll so that the reverse side of st st is on the outside. Catch together cast-on edge to cast-off edge in the direction that they have rolled. Sew in any loose ends.

Legs (make 2)
Cast on 12sts in tan, 2sts in pink or a contrast colour.
Work 6 rows stocking st.
Cast off 14sts.
Catch and sew edges as for the Arms.

Body
Cast on 20sts in cream.
Work 17 rows in st st.
Then knit 6 rows more.
Cast off.

Head
Cast on 4sts in tan or skin tone.
Row 1: Knit.
Row 2: Purl.
Row 3: Knit, inc 1 st at either end of row. (6sts)
Row 4: Purl.
Repeat rows 3 and 4 (8 sts).
Work 4 rows more in stocking st.

ROW 11: Knit, dec 1 st at either end or row. (6sts)
ROW 12: Purl.
ROWS 13 & 14: As rows 10 and 11. (4sts)
ROW 15: Purl.
ROW 16: Knit.
Cast off.

Wings (make 2)

Wings are all garter st (knit every row).
Cast on 6sts in cream.
ROWS 1 & 2: Knit.
ROW 3: Knit, inc 1 st at either end of row. (10sts)
ROW 4: Cast on 4 sts at beg of row, knit to end. (14sts)
Work 3 rows in garter st.
ROWS 8–11: Rep last 4 rows. (18sts)
ROW 12: Cast on 4sts at beg of row, knit to end. (22sts)
ROW 13: Knit, dec 1 st at beg of row.
ROW 14: Knit, dec 1 st at end of row.
ROW 15: Knit, dec 1 st at beg of row. (19sts)
Cast off (this is the outside edge of your wing).

Skirt

Cast on 44sts in cream and knit 2 rows.
ROW 3: Knit.
ROW 4: Purl.
ROWS 5–18: Rep rows 3 and 4, ending on a purl row.
ROW 19: K4, k2tog, * k3, k2tog, rep from * 6 times more, k3.
(36sts)
ROW 20: Purl.
ROW 21: K3, k2tog, * k2, k2tog, rep from * 6 times more, k3.
(28sts)
ROW 22: Purl.
ROW 20: K2, k2tog, * k1, k2tog, rep from * 6 times more, k3.
(20sts)
ROW 21: Purl.
Cast off.
Fold in half and sew the side seam of the skirt.

To make up

♥ For the head, sew side seams, then stuff from base.
Embroider eyes with two small over stitches (see page 226)
for each.

♥ To make hair, thread a darning needle with yellow yarn
and stitch around the head with random running stitch (see
page 226) but leaving loops instead of pulling the yarn flat.

♥ For the body, fold in half and catch the legs at each corner
of the cast-on edge and sew across with running stitch,
securing the legs in position as you sew. Sew the side seam
of the body, then stuff the body and sew approximately 5mm
(¼in) either side on cast-off edge for shoulders.

♥ Attach the base of the head to the 'neck' space, using
over stitch or a neat stitch as preferred.

♥ Place the skirt over the doll's body and use over stitch to
catch the cast-off edge around the body approximately 1cm
(½in) below the garter st detail of the body.

♥ Sew in any loose ends

♥ To attach the wings, sew the cast-on edge of each wing to
the centre back of the angel's body.

Decorating for
Christmas

CLEARLY, EVERYONE HAS their own 'look' or style when it comes to decorating the house for Christmas: the following sums up ours. Feel free to adapt or expand on these suggestions as you will, using whatever materials and treasured decorations you have to hand. What feels important is to simplify: fewer shop-bought decorations means less expense and hassle. Making things from natural objects and materials found around the house and garden can become part of the life-enchancing rituals leading up to Christmas, especially if children are able to lend a hand. Freeing oneself from some of the commerciality of Christmas leaves room for the truly fundamental aspects of the festive period: acknowledging its spiritual significance in whatever way seems to chime with our beliefs and relishing time spent with friends and family.

Festive mantelpiece

There are all sorts of fancy Christmas decorations for sale in the shops, but to our mind, nothing can beat the traditional favourites, starting out with natural materials and adding fairy lights and treasured items as you will. Build a roaring fragrant fire in the grate beneath and you are really ready for Father Christmas.

You will need

- Trailing ivy (can be pruned from garden)
- Sprigs of holly
- Fir cones, berries and other woodland items, perhaps gathered on a winter's walk
- Set of fairy lights
- Baubles and other favourite decorations

To decorate the mantelpiece

♥ It is best to clear and dust your shelf or mantelpiece first, before draping the ivy in swags, anchoring them with the heavier sprigs of holly and punctuating with fir cones, bright berries and other natural objects.

♥ Weave a set of fairy lights in among the foliage – plain white or red-hot chilli pepper lights look best for Christmas.

♥ Add a few baubles, other special decorations or cards as you see fit. It can be nice to give homemade cards some recognition by displaying them in a prominent place.

♥ A real fire in the grate is the true finishing touch. Stack plenty of wood alongside for a feeling of warmth and security, whatever the weather; maybe try to track down apple or pear wood, which burn with a gloriously atmospheric scent.

Felt decorations

Bursting with cheerful colour and homespun charm, these felt decorations (see below and overleaf) couldn't be simpler, and are a great way of involving children in pre-Christmas preparations. They could even make decorations to give as presents to friends, godparents and teachers, slipped in with a homemade Christmas card. The selection of patterns overleaf is really just a guide – you can copy some, but also feel free to get creative with other Christmassy images, such as crowns, snowmen and ivy leaves, as the mood takes you. Mix them with other traditional decorations on the tree or, if you prefer, show them off on their own on bare twiggy branches in a jug (in the spirit of the Easter tree on page 32), laid along the mantelpiece or strung up as a mobile.

How much time and effort you spend on each decoration is up to you. The quickest option is just to use running stitch (see page 225) around the edge, or you can decorate the felt with embroidery stitches as shown opposite. For instructions on embroidery stitches, see pages 225–6.

Add sequins (as for the Christmas tree opposite) or lightly stuff the felt shapes (with shredded old tights or kapok) to make three-dimensional decorations (as in the ivy and orange star). For the stockings, why not embroider names or short messages? A selection of these decorations could also be put in the pockets of the Advent calendar on page 202.

You will need

◆ Felt, which is generally much cheaper when sold by the metre than in smaller squares
◆ Ribbon (ideally recycled lengths from your ribbon stash, see page 206)
◆ Sewing threads in contrasting colours to felt
◆ Sequins (optional)

To make

♥ Using a paper pattern only where really necessary (but you may find the outlines given on page 241 helpful), cut out the decorations, using two layers of felt for each one. As with our heart (see page 215), you might choose to cut out some of the pieces of felt with pinking shears to add a pretty, deckled edging.

♥ Sew around the edge with tiny running stitches in a contrasting colour to create a basic but attractive decoration, securing a loop of pretty ribbon as you sew, at the top edge with the running stitch.

♥ To make the decorations illustrated here, follow the instructions to the right. Or feel free to be led by your own creative urges.

Star, heart and stocking

♥ These three lovely decorations are shown in the photograph on page 215. We used chain stitch to decorate the star, heart and stocking (spelling 'Noel' on the star, 'PAX' on the heart and for the hem edge of the stocking cuff).

♥ For the stocking, before sewing together the two main pieces, work a row of chain stitch across the bottom edge of the white cuff, attaching it to the stocking.

♥ Sew around the outside edge of the stocking with running stitch, but leave the top open, and attach the ribbon loop to the corner of the top back edge. Work a row of running stitches around the top of the stocking to secure the white cuff in place while allowing space for a chocolate or spiral sugar cane to be inserted into the stocking.

Bauble and holly leaf

♥ For the bauble, sew around the outside with running stitch, leaving a space about 2cm (¾in) wide to add stuffing. After stuffing, continue sewing up the gap with running stitch, adding the ribbon loop for hanging.

♥ For the holly (pictured right), sew the veins of the leaves with small back stitches, then sew two or three small circles of felt (for the berries) to the top near the ribbon.

Adding sequins

We sewed sequins to the bauble and Christmas tree. Using a continuous thread, add the sequins randomly all over the decoration, passing the thread between both pieces of felt to hide it. Or you could add the sequins before stitching the felt together.

Dressing the Christmas tree

Dressing the Christmas tree is a lovely ritual in which all the family can participate. Choose a time when you can work in an unhurried way – ideally towards the end of the afternoon or early evening so that the lights can be switched on with a degree of ceremony when it gets dark.

The idea of the 'styled' tree, with all the objects newly bought to fit in with an agreed colour scheme is anathema to the *Homemade* approach. Instead, bring out vintage decorations that have become family heirlooms since your own childhood and beyond, plus newer ones made by hand, perhaps some of them by the children in your life. Homemade, handmade items bring an energy all of their own to the tree, adding to its significance as a family talisman, loaded with memories and associations, from year to year.

Like the eggs on the Easter tree (see page 32), your collection of tree decorations will become a treasured possession, which you can add to year by year. As well as handmade pieces, such as the embroidered felt shapes on the previous page, we also buy a few new or second-hand items every so often – from vintage finds on eBay to those picked up on trips around the country or travels abroad.

Less is most definitely less when it comes to tree decoration. In our book, you can't have enough decorations and we load our trees with this eclectic mix of old and new until there is very little greenery showing in between.

We try to buy sustainable, non-dropping trees. Elspeth also has a smaller tree, bought for her daughter three years ago, which goes out into the garden in its pot after Twelfth Night, is kept well watered so the bushy new light green growth comes through each spring, and can be brought inside and decorated in the early days of December with miniature handmade paper chains and other treasured items.

When it comes to taking down the decorations on the traditional time of Twelfth Night (6 January or Epiphany), make this a meaningful event, too. Put on the Christmas music for one last time, eat up those remaining mince pies and slices of Christmas cake, and savour the experience. Take time to wrap the decorations carefully, putting them away in mouse- and moth-proof containers, and look through your card collection one more time, saving any homemade ones that might provide inspiration for another year and cutting up other for *Homemade* tags next year. And give thanks in your heart for all the Christmases past and ones yet to come.

Handmade items bring an energy all of their own to the tree, adding to its significance as a family talisman, loaded with memories and associations, from year to year.

homemade
basics

Homemade craft basics

Whether it's making cards, wrapping presents, labelling homemade produce or dealing with fiddly details, such as lining the Easter trug (see page 50) or fixing the patchwork fabric on the Denim chair (see page 68), having a well-stocked crafts kit at the ready can help everything go smoothly. Not having to hunt around the house to locate the right type of glue, roll of sticky tape and so on will allow your creativity full rein, ensuring that your project will turn out the best it can possibly be.

Our own crafts kits are a combination of bought stuff – tried-and-tested glues, paints and other products that we know will give a good performance – and goodies that we have saved from here and there, happy in the knowledge that they will be given another life in some creative project or other. We save everything, from pretty wrapping paper (larger areas only and with the creases ironed out where necessary) to rubber bands, ribbons from presents or bouquets of flowers – even the coloured cotton tape from the heavy paper bags that are increasingly given away in clothes and other shops instead of plastic bags.

A large drawer can be handy for storing these items, with boxes or dividers within it to keep everything sorted. Also useful are mini chests of drawers made from wood or cardboard that can be stacked up next to or on top of one another and added to when required. Or you might prefer something more idiosyncratic to contain your kit, such as a sturdy reclaimed wicker laundry basket with old biscuit tins housing all the bits inside, or a series of lovely old leather suitcases of varying sizes. The important thing is to have a system that works efficiently and looks pleasing into the bargain.

The Homemade craft kit

✳ Different types of glue for paper, fabric and wood, and Superglue for fiddly items.
✳ Sticky tape and double-sided tape.
✳ Masking tape.
✳ Roll of brown parcel paper.
✳ Stick-on plain white labels of various sizes.
✳ Lead pencils.
✳ Coloured crayons.
✳ Set of felt pens.
✳ Fountain pen and ink.
✳ Staple gun.
✳ Drawing pins.
✳ Tacks
✳ Hammer.
✳ Paper (coloured and white).

For wrapping presents

✳ Brown parcel paper.
✳ Newsprint and magazine paper.
✳ Tissue paper in a variety of colours.
✳ Rescued/reused wrapping paper sorted into larger pieces for reuse and smaller pieces for strips and borders (if you can find time to iron out creases, the paper will look heaps better).
✳ String.
✳ Raffia.
✳ Reels of new ribbon in one or two key colours. Red, for example, can perk up newsprint or brown paper and silver is good for use with tissue paper or even coloured magazine pages.
✳ Silver paint, which is good for painting stars, names and other adornments.
✳ Silver and gold pens.
✳ Pompoms and other embellishments that are easy to use and will perk up plainer wrapping.
✳ Old-fashioned brown paper luggage labels in various sizes or scraps of cardboard for making your own labels.

And for painting projects

✳ Primer/undercoat for dark and light colours.
✳ Outdoor and indoor eggshell paint: preferably water-based for ease of use and lower chemical content.
✳ White spirit: for cleaning brushes if using non-water-based paints.
✳ Brushes in various sizes, from 5–7.5cm (2–3in) wide for covering larger areas to pointed artist's brushes for handpainting.
✳ Fabric paints and/or fabric crayons.
✳ Erasible pencil/chalk for marking out projects.

Sewing kit basics

It is good to have two sewing kits: one can be small and portable, containing the bare essentials (needles, thread, safety pins and a spare button or two) that you keep in a handbag and use for mending on the go, and the other much more extensive – based at home and used for larger projects, such as those in this book. The following items are recommended for inclusion in the latter.

The Homemade sewing kit

✳ Basic sewing machine (not essential but certainly useful) and a variety of sewing machine needles.

✳ Two pairs at least of sharp scissors: small, very sharp embroidery scissors (good for unpicking) and a good-quality pair of fabric shears. By including both pairs of scissors, you are ensuring that the fabric scissors will last a long time. Ideally, you would also include a medium pair of scissors for cutting paper patterns. Never using your sewing scissors for paper makes them stay sharp much longer.

✳ Pinking shears for making zigzag edges to hems (less likely to fray) and cutting fabrics such as felt in an attractive way. Their name comes from the common pink, in the genus Dianthus, or carnation, which has scalloped edges to its petals.

✳ Pins stuck in an attractive Handmade pincushion if possible (see page 170), though magnetic pin holders are also available. Many people find quilting pins with coloured heads easier to handle, and they are certainly easier to see, making it less likely that you will leave pins in place on a finished item. The larger headed pins are particularly useful when working with knitting or crochet, as conventional pins get lost easily and can slip out of place in a loose open-weave structure.

✳ Hand-sewing needles in various sizes, including thicker darning needles for working with thicker thread or wool.

✳ Safety pins, fastened together for safety and convenience.

✳ Tailor's chalk for marking out patterns (this washes or brushes out easily).

✳ Cotton thread in various colours; a multi-coloured skein is handy for a smaller kit, but more commonly used colours, such as black, white and navy, are as well kept in longer reels.

✳ Tape measure that reads in imperial and metric. One that retracts inside a leather or Bakelite cover is useful and less likely to get damaged or lost.

✳ Poppers and hooks and eyes for fastening.

✳ Fusible fabric, such as Bondaweb.

✳ Button box (see page 142) containing buttons of all shapes, colours and sizes.

✳ Rag bag full of scraps and smaller pieces of fabric that you have saved up over the years.

✳ Steam iron for pressing fabric before, during and after making up.

Non-essentials, but useful

✳ Thimble, especially if you get sore fingers and thumbs.

✳ Seam ripper/unpicker.

✳ Ruler to provide a more solid edge than a tape measure.

✳ Embroidery threads in all colours.

✳ Tapestry wool for thicker embroidery and embellishments.

Where you keep your sewing equipment depends largely on the size of your kit and how much space is available in your home. Some people have an entire room of the house devoted to sewing and/or other crafts, with cupboards and drawers stuffed full of fabrics and coloured thread. Others have just a small bag or box; perhaps a patchwork bag that has been specially made for the purpose, or a traditional box with hinged side sections that lift out. An ideal in-between option is a shelf or section of a cupboard, just for your sewing goodies.

What is important for motivational as well as practical reasons is that the kit should be well organized and attractively laid out. Make or buy handmade pin cushions and needle books for keeping sharp items safe; those made by children are often particularly charming. Save pretty old tins and jars for keeping other small items ordered.

Learning to sew

For more on courses and learning how to sew, see the Directory on page 243.

Basic stitches used in this book

Most of the instructions below and overleaf are based on those supplied on the website of the Embroiderer's Guild (www.embroiderersguild.com/stitch/stitches/). There are also some superb YouTube entries, some of which show the creation of the stitches very clearly, accompanied by music!

1 Back stitch

Bring the thread up through the fabric on the stitch line and then take a small backward stitch down through the fabric. Bring the needle through again a little in front of the first stitch, then take another backwards stitch, inserting the needle at the point where it first came through.

2 Blanket stitch

Push the needle up through the fabric a short way from the edge, hooking the rest of the thread around the top of the needle. Pull the needle through the fabric, keeping the lower thread out of the way so the thread forms a loop around the edge of the fabric. Repeat to create a line of linked stitches along the fabric edge.

3 Chain stitch

Having pulled the needle through the fabric, insert the needle next to where it emerged and bring the point out a short distance away. Pull the thread around the needle, keeping it under the needle's point, and pull the needle through the fabric to create a looped stitch. Holding down the loop, repeat to make a series of linked chains.

4 Cross stitch

Working on the canvas holes in groups of four, bring the needle up through the lower left hole (1) and take it down through the canvas one hole up and to the right (2). Bring it through to the front again one hole down (3) to form a half cross. Continue in this way to the end of the row, then complete the upper section of the cross. Cross stitch can be worked from left to right, as shown, or from right to left, but it is important that the upper half of each cross lies in one direction.

Cross-stitch fabric or Binca (used for making the Cross-stich no entry sign on page 184) comes in different 'counts' (for example, 'six count' means six holes per inch) and in a variety of colours. Start with a low-count fabric as your work will progress quicker and it is easier to use. You can buy it direct from www.threadsite.co.uk/tandem/fabrics/binca.html.

1
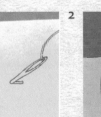

2
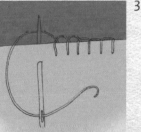

3
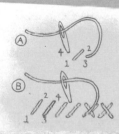

4
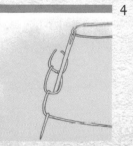

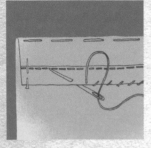

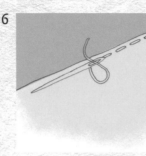

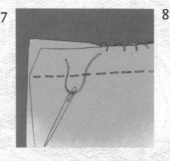

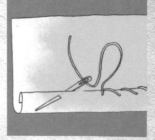

5 Hem stitch

Fold the hem horizontally with your thumb on the hem. Lay the end of your thread in the fold of the hem. Working from left to right, take a small back stitch through just the hem to anchor the thread. Moving a small way along the fabric to the right, pick up two threads from the work and pull gently. Then pick up two threads from the folded hem, to the right of the first stitch. Move on to the next two threads in the work, pull gently and then pick up two threads in the hem. Continue working in this way towards the corner.

6 Running stitch

Pass the needle in and out of the fabric, making sure that the surface stitches are of equal length. The stitches on the underside should also be of equal length, but half the size or less than the upper stitches.

7 Over stitch

This stitch is worked from the right side and is often used to join together pieces of fabric, or as an alternative to blanket stitch to prevent fraying. Place the pieces of work together with wrong sides facing, then bring the needle up through both layers from the underside. Repeat, always bringing the needle from the underside of the work. The thread binds together the two layers of fabric. Over stitch is especially useful for joining the fabric for a stuffed toy.

8 Slip stitch

A slip stitch can be used to repair a seam from the top. Push a threaded needle (be sure to knot the thread) through the material on one side of the opening, and then on the other. Continue until the seam is closed.

Making a buttonhole

These instructions tell you how to make a buttonhole using any sewing machine that can make a zigzag. If you have a newer machine, with fancy pre-programmed buttonhole settings, you don't need to do it this way. Or you can handstitch by sewing around the open hole initially using over stitch and then buttonhole stitch, which is basically blanket stitch worked very closely together (see page 225). Neatly done, a hand-sewn buttonhole is a work of art. Most buttonholes are made with thread that matches the fabric colour. Stick to that convention for any machine-sewn buttonholes, as no matter how well these are done they will be functional rather than decorative. For buttonholes beautiful enough to be a feature, hand-sewn or bound buttonholes are the answer.

✳ Mark out your buttonholes with tailor's chalk. They should be at least 5mm (¼in) larger than the buttons you intend to use. As a rule, buttonholes should be parallel with the edge of the garment so the button will pull on the end of the buttonhole, not the middle, where it would gap and look strange. The traditional marking is shaped like a capital 'I', which emphasizes where the ends are so all of the buttonholes end up the same length.

✳ On the sewing machine, set your stitch width to maximum and your stitch length to 0 to create a wide zigzag that isn't going anywhere fast.

✳ Position the needle at the furthest end of the buttonhole marking. Stitch five or six zigzags to create the bar at that end of the buttonhole, finishing with your needle on the left. (Don't pull the fabric out or cut the thread after this stage – you want the thread to be taut between steps.)

✳ Set the stitch width to half of the maximum value and increase the stitch length a little. Stitch down the length of the buttonhole to the other end. Once again, don't pull the fabric out or cut the thread after this stage.

✳ Reset your stitch width to maximum and your stitch length to '0'. Reposition the needle so its centre position matches the centre line of the buttonhole.

✳ Make five or seven zigzags at that end of the buttonhole. Be sure to do an odd number, so you end up with the needle at the extreme right. Leave the needle down and turn the entire garment around by 180 degrees.

✳ Once again, set the stitch width to half the maximum value and increase the stitch length a tiny bit. Position the needle so that its leftmost position matches the leftmost extent of the stitching just completed.

✳ Stitch down the length of the buttonhole back to where you started, being careful to stay parallel to the first side you sewed. Let the zigzag go a little into the starting zigzag for added strength.

✳ Using either buttonhole scissors, a seam unpicker or ordinary sewing scissors, carefully cut open the buttonhole. Make sure you don't cut the stitching, particularly at the ends. Snip any loose threads and try passing the button through the hole.

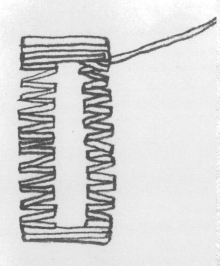

Knitting basics

By far the best way to learn knitting is one-on-one from a more experienced friend or relative. But there are also many groups and drop-in 'clinics' around, so for further information check out the Directory on page 245. The excellent website www.dominknitrix.com includes a gallery of pictures to help you learn various stitches, mattress stitch included.

The *Homemade* knitting kit

✳ A selection of knitting needles in different sizes: the ones in the book are size 2.75mm (UK size 12; US size 2) (Decorated coat hangers and iPod cover, see pages 36 and 136), 3.25mm (UK size 10; US size 3) (Fingerless gloves, see page 188), 4.5mm (UK size 7; US size 7) (Tea cosy, see page 138) and 6.5mm (UK size 3; US size 10½) (Woolly scarf, see page 186).
✳ Various crochet hooks of different sizes: handy for finishing off some of the knitting projects, such as the coat hanger and iPod covers (size 2mm and 2.5mm).
✳ Tape measure: ideally a retractable one in an attractive case.
✳ Small sharp scissors: embroidery scissors are ideal.
✳ Pencil and paper: for notes and making impromptu patterns.
✳ Stitch holder: at least one, for holding stitches when changing needles.
✳ Safety pins of various sizes.
✳ Needle gauge: for checking needle sizes.
✳ Circular needles: for making socks and gloves.
✳ Darning needles: for sewing flat pieces of knitting together.
✳ Button box (see page 142).
✳ Selection of small scraps of knitting yarn for embroidery and darning: these can be kept in a pretty tin or bag.

Most people keep knitting and crochet materials together as so many of the materials and pieces of equipment are duplicated, and crochet details are often used to finish off a knitting project. However, once a particular project is on the go, you may want to keep just the things pertaining to that item in the bag you keep with you at all times. It would help, therefore, to have separate knitting and crochet kits and include more than one of some of the items listed.

Knitting can be kept in anything from a large old biscuit tin to a decorative bag made specially for the purpose, with different-sized pockets for needles, wool and so on. Or how about storing your knitting and crochet needles in a fishing tackle box? The small compartments can be used for darning needles, quilting pins, safety pins and any other bits of paraphernalia that you have. What you choose will depend partly on your own sense of style and partly on the size of your knitting projects – a crocheted blanket will take up more space than a pair of fingerless gloves, for instance.

Choosing yarn

Different yarns give different results: smooth and silky or rough and hairy. Long filaments create a different effect compared to short ones – compare the difference between an item made with a loose yarn, such as mohair, and one made with a tightly twisted yarns, such as mercerized cotton. So take all this into account when choosing yarn for a project.

Whatever yarn you choose, try to make it the best possible quality. After all the time and love you put into making something, you don't want it to look tired, misshapen and bobbly after only one wash.

Buying good knitting yarn now is a treat not a trauma. Gone are the days of scratchy wool and acrylic in nasty colours, and though the demise of the corner wool shop has been sad, the internet has made sourcing much easier in recent years. Numerous companies (see the Directory, pages 245–6) make beautiful ranges of pure and mixed yarn and have pure wool that washes well and feels soft and wearable.

The main problem is price: good yarn can be very expensive. Shop around for bargains, especially on the internet. There are hundreds of online yarn stores and, of course, eBay, all selling beautiful yarns at knockdown prices. Check out the brand first at your local wool shop or department store and then look it up online and see what you can find.

We have used mercerized cotton in this book for the coat hanger and iPod covers (see pages 36 and 136). This has a slight sheen to it, due to it being highly spun in manufacture. Ordinary 4-ply will make up the same pattern in the same way, but won't have the same luxurious look. When a pattern is using so little yarn, we think it is worth using mercerized instead of matt cotton to get the best possible effect.

Yarn usually comes in 50g (2oz) balls but, for economy, try to find yarn on large hanks, or larger still 500g (1lb 2oz) cones, which are a cheaper option when buying new.

Quite often yarn is reduced if it is an odd dye lot (see 'Notes' right) and this is worth buying to add to your store when knitting or crocheting things that use small quantities, such as the Crochet squares (see page 180), Decorated coat hangers (see page 36), Fingerless gloves (see page 188) and Tea cosy (see page 138).

The make-do-and-mend mentality of the post-war generation meant it was common for people to unravel and re-knit their jerseys, steaming the wool to take out the kinks. While we wouldn't advocate this as essential, it certainly makes sense financially, provided you have time, the next time your child outgrows a nice hand-knit or you see an item made from a lovely yarn but don't like the style.

Knitting terms

UK yarns are specified in ply, but this and other terms are different in the US:

UK	US
4-ply	Sportweight
Doubleknitting	Worsted
Aran	Fisherman or medium weight
Chunky	Bulky

Notes for knitters

✳ ALWAYS work a tension swatch, no matter how little time you have. Then check it against the pattern and change your needles accordingly if necessary.
✳ The knitting and crochet tensions quoted on all the patterns in this book are a guide only. Every knitter has a personal tension – whether tight or loose.
✳ To check your tension, knit a square to the size given in the pattern and using the stitch from the pattern. When the square is complete, lay it on a flat surface and, using a tape measure, count the number of stitches and then the number of rows.
✳ If you have more stitches or rows than the tension indicated, use slightly smaller needles. If you have fewer stitches or rows, try using larger needles.
✳ The above also means that some knitters may use more or less yarn than that quoted.
✳ If buying more than one ball of the same-coloured yarn, make sure they all have the same batch number – this is printed on the ball band. Although they may look the same to the naked eye, the same colour from different dye batches will always show on the finished piece and spoil the uniform effect.
✳ When it's time to put your knitting away, pop a cork on the end of needles to stop the stitches falling off.
✳ Never leave your knitting in the middle of a row or there may be an obviously larger stitch in the middle once it is finished.

Abbreviations used for the Homemade projects
cont continue
col colour
dec decrease/decreasing
inc increase/increasing
k knit
MC main colour
p purl
rep repeat
RS right side
st/sts stitches
tog together

Crochet basics

In Victorian times up until the mid 20th century, crochet was used extensively for making and decorating clothes and household items. Children were taught to knit and crochet at school, but like knitting it fell out of fashion and the skill has been more widely lost in recent years. The huge resurgence in knitting, however, has led to crochet becoming another skill that people interested in handicrafts are keen to learn.

Crochet is as simple as knitting, some find it is easier. Ros learned to crochet before she could knit (she was only seven), and her first project was a doll's blanket. Just as with knitting, there are lots of different crochet stitches that can vary the look and texture of your work. Some styles are easier to achieve with crochet than with knitting; for instance, the undulating pattern of the crochet coat hanger cover on page 38 would be much harder to achieve if knitted.

Just Google 'how to crochet' and you'll find thousands of websites packed with advice and able to teach you everything you need to get started. Because crochet used to be so popular, there are lots of amazing vintage patterns about – good sources include www.annalaia.com/ or www.knitting-crochet.com/crochet/antiquecrochet.html. Alternatively, try eBay or your local thrift shop; the latter will probably have a box of old patterns – anyone for a crochet bikini?

One of the oddest patterns Ros came across has to be one for crochet sleeves for your piano legs. She also has a pattern for a pair of crochet indoor sandals and recently saw a pattern for a baby's bottle cover. Vintage patterns that could easily become stylish, trendy and covetable include the many for crochet flowers and jewellery.

The *Homemade* crochet kit

✳ A selection of crochet hooks of different sizes. The ones used in this book are 2mm and 2.5mm (the coat hanger and iPod covers, see pages 38 and 136).
✳ Tape measure: ideally a retractable one in an attractive case.
✳ Small sharp scissors: embroidery scissors are ideal.
✳ Pencil and paper: for notes and making impromptu patterns.
✳ Stitch holder: at least one – for holding stitches when changing hooks.
✳ Safety pins of various sizes.
✳ Darning needles: for sewing together flat pieces of crochet.
✳ Button box (see page 142).
✳ Selection of small scraps of knitting yarn for embroidery or darning: these can be kept in a pretty tin or bag within the bag.

Most items for crochet tend to be smaller than those for knitting – and the hooks are smaller than needles for a start – so the chances are that your crochet kit will fit into a smaller box, bag or tin than the *Homemade* knitting kit listed on page 228. Whether you choose a zip-up or closed-hinge receptacle rather than an open one depends largely on whether you will be taking your kit out with you (on the bus or train or even to the cinema), or keeping it at home, and whether you need to keep your work and yarn protected from the ravages of children and/or pets. Choose something attractive, though, which will help you keep your work in order and make you want to pick it up often.

Choosing yarn

Traditionally, crochet yarn is a fine cotton, tightly twisted to avoid splitting. It gives a firmer finish to your work than other yarns, which was important for household objects that were commonly crocheted from mid 1800 to around 1950, and are still produced today by artisans in some European and south American countries. The yarn is still available and is usually referred to as crochet cotton. This fine cotton is best suited to lace work and – unless you are working from a vintage pattern, making something like traditional table linens (hardly likely if you are a beginner) – is far too fine for contemporary patterns and styles. Although you may be making small crochet flowers in the traditional manner, working from a contemporary colour palette would make them into incredibly fashionable accessories.

Ros tends to use knitting yarns in all her crochet work as the patterns require thicker yarns. It is vital that the yarn you choose is appropriate for the design and that you avoid anything knobbly or with a slub, as these cause problems when working stitches together, common in crochet patterns.

See also Knitting basics (pages 228–9).

Crochet terms

European and US stitches are the same, but other crochet terms differ.

UK	US
Cast off	Fasten off
Double crochet (dc)	Single crochet (sc)
Double treble	Treble (tr)
Miss	Skip
Tension	Gauge
Treble (tr)	Double crochet (dc)
Work straight	Work even

Notes for crocheters

See also Knitting basics (pages 228–9).

Abbreviations used in the Homemade ideas
ch chain
dc double crochet
sl st slip stitch
sp space
tr treble

Hook sizes

Crochet hooks are made from aluminium, plastic, bamboo or sometimes bone. European and US hook sizes also differ and since 1970 have been as follows (for pre-1970 hooks look at www.antiquepatternlibrary.org/vintagehooks.htm):

Steel hooks		Aluminum hooks	
mm range	US range*	mm range	US range*
.75mm	14	2.25mm	B-1
.85mm	13	2.75mm	C-2
1mm	12	3.25mm	D-3
1.1mm	11	3.5mm	E-4
1.3mm	10	3.75mm	F-5
1.4mm	9	4mm	G-6
1.5mm	8	4.5mm	7
1.65mm	7	5mm	H-8
1.8mm	6	5.5mm	I-9
1.9mm	5	6mm	J-10
2mm	4	6.5mm	K-101/2
2.1mm	3	8mm	L-11
2.25mm	2	9mm	M/N-13
2.75mm	1	10mm	N/P-15
3.25mm	0	15mm	P/Q
3.5mm	00	16mm	Q
		19mm	S

* The letter or number may vary, so rely on the millimetre (mm) sizing.

Cooking basics

Cooking with the right equipment is almost as important as using the right ingredients. Apart from a bustling sense of efficiency that really helps everything along, a good cooking kit can add immeasurably to the pleasures of the task in hand. A heavy glass bowl, possibly with a lip for pouring, in which to whisk eggs; the correct-size cake tins and baking trays; a pretty cooling rack and fun, well-made cookie cutters can all contribute to good cake-making, while unusual jars and bottles and good labels and pens are essential for finishing jams and chutneys in style.

The *Homemade* baking kit

✳ Mixing bowls: for mixing cake ingredients and incorporating the air that helps them rise. A set of nesting ones may be an attractive and useful option.

✳ Wooden spoons for mixing.

✳ Large metal spoons for folding in flour.

✳ Rubber spatulas for scraping bowls clean.

✳ Cooking tins for cakes and baking trays for scones and biscuits (see right).

✳ Wire balloon whisk for beating air into eggs and/or an electric hand whisk (the purists swear by the former, but the latter makes life easier and quicker).

✳ Wire cooling racks for allowing air to circulate all around cakes when they come out of the oven. If stood on a flat surface, the bases can go soggy.

✳ Glass measuring jug: for measuring liquid ingredients at a glance.

✳ Rolling pin: an old-fashioned wooden (or even marble) rolling pin is indispensable for rolling out the marzipan for our Simnel cake (see page 58), not to mention pastry.

✳ Plain and fluted cutters: for small cakes, biscuits and scones. Never twist the cutter as you cut – just press down once and remove. Twisting can make for very strange shapes.

✳ Palette knife: useful for loosening cakes, including lifting cup cakes from cake tins and scones from baking trays.

✳ Nylon piping bag with one or two plain or starred nozzles for cake decorations – or buy ready-made icing in nozzle tubes.

✳ Wire or plastic sieves: for sifting the likes of flour and icing sugar to remove lumps and allow air in.

✳ Good scales are essential for baking and jam making. Proper balance scales may be expensive, but they do last a lifetime; cheap, flimsy spring scales with needle indicators will not, and often work out more expensive in the long run.

Tips for good cake making

✳ Get out all your ingredients before you start. Not only do you know for sure that you have them all; it will also make you feel calmer and more organized – a feeling that only contributes to good cooking. Most importantly, this practice should also bring all the ingredients to room temperature before you start.

✳ Preheat the oven so it is at the required temperature before you put the filled cake tin in to bake.

✳ Use good-quality cake tins of the right size for the recipe (see below).

✳ Cool thoroughly on a wire rack.

Cake tins

It is important to use good cake tins, and to use the correct size – even half an inch difference in diameter can upset the cooking times and the overall appearance and texture of the cake. The tins specified in this book are a standard size, cupcake patty tins and baking trays that can be found in any reasonably stocked kitchen shop or department store. Quality is important, as the heavier they are, the less likely they are to burn – plus they last longer. The depth is especially important for sponge tins, as without any depth above it, the cake won't rise: use a sponge tin that is at least 4cm (1½in) deep. Many people complain about flat sponges when it wasn't the recipe that was the problem; it was that the sponge had nowhere to go.

Non-stick tins are definitely easiest to use, though one is never too sure of all those chemicals used in the manufacturing process, and they can let you down sometimes. Non-stick springform tins – hinged so that the cake simply pops free when done – are the best by far. Once you have used one, you will never go back to the old-fashioned sort. Always grease and line any cake tin, non-stick or otherwise, just to be sure that the finished cake comes away easily, without getting stuck and/or broken in the process.

Lining and greasing a round tin

✳ Grease the cake tin with the same sort of fat as is used in the recipe, smearing it evenly all over the inside of the tin and into any corners, if there are any. Keep folded-up butter papers in the fridge door for this purpose, smearing more butter on if necessary.

✳ Cut a strip of parchment paper slightly longer than the circumference of the tin and 7.5cm (3in) higher than its depth. Fold the paper back about 2.5cm (1in) along its length, then snip it at an angle at intervals up to the fold.

✳ Press the paper around the sides of the tin so the snipped edge overlaps the base of the tin for a snug fit.

✳ Cut out a circle of parchment paper – using the tin as a template – to fit over the snipped paper over the base. Grease again lightly with fat. For extra crispness on the outside of the cake, sprinkle the tin with flour.

Care of cake tins

Some people never wash their cake tins, simply wiping them to avoid rust. The best way to take care of them, however, is to wash in hot water and dry well immediately afterwards, leaving on a radiator or near an Aga or Rayburn just to make sure all the moisture has been banished before storing away in a cupboard.

Storing cakes

There is nothing nicer than a row of pretty, well-stocked cake tins in your larder or ranged along your kitchen shelf. They are preferable to plastic boxes for practical as well as aesthetic reasons as metal is non-porous and cannot harbour smells and bacteria in the way that plastic can, however carefully you wash it.

Be careful if you are tempted by old tins in thrift shops, however, as they often have rust on them, which can contaminate the cakes and smell.

Also do not be tempted to store cakes and biscuits in the same tin, as the moisture from the cakes will make the biscuits soggy. For short-term storage, wrap cakes in aluminium foil, but if you're storing a rich fruit cake, such as the Simnel cake on page 58, for a longer period, then use a double layer of greaseproof paper on the inside and foil on the outside – the acid in the fruit can corrode the foil if it comes into direct contact with it and cause mould.

Sterilizing jars and bottles

Sterilized jars and bottles are absolutely crucial for storing jams, jellies, sloe gin and elderflower cordial if they are not to be at risk from going mouldy. The traditional method for sterilizing involves scrubbing the jars well in warm soapy water, rinsing in clean water and placing them to dry in a cool oven (140°C/275°F/Gas 1). But glass that is hot and clean from a dishwasher is pretty much sterile, and this is a lot less demanding – even if you have to time the cycle to be ready when you need the jars, as it is important that they should be filled when hot.

Alternatively, sterilize the jars and bottles in a microwave by filling each jar a quarter full with water and microwaving on high for 10 minutes – again, use while warm.

Jam will benefit from circles of greaseproof paper being placed over the surface of the jam – this further prevents contamination, but be sure to wash your hands scrupulously first.

Jam-making tips

✳ Always use a stainless steel pan rather than an aluminium one as aluminium may react with the acid in the fruit. Buy as large a pan as possible as, when the mixture comes to the 'rolling boil' required for setting, it will rise way up the sides of the pan.

✳ A good heavy bottom to the pan will also help prevent burning.

Gardening basics

If you have a large garden or go the whole hog and take on an allotment, you will no doubt have a shed full of gardening paraphernalia. But for those who are just starting out, and fancy a foray into some of the simpler gardening projects outlined in this book, such as the Easter trug (see page 50), Recycled containers (see page 84), here are a few suggestions. The information on sowing seeds (see page 44) contains all you need for getting your own seedlings started.

The *Homemade* gardening kit

✳ Hand trowel: for digging holes and spooning out compost.
✳ Hand fork: for weeding and dividing larger plants into smaller ones for filling containers, such as violas for the Easter trug and the Summer salad trough (see page 110).
✳ Secateurs: for removing any dead or dying material.
✳ Scissors: for above, plus snipping string and any labelling needs.
✳ Hammer and nails: for repairing reclaimed containers and knocking holes in the base of recycled containers.
✳ Electric drill: for making holes in more resistant containers.
✳ Garden wire and twine: for tying up plants and guiding plants to supports or trellis.
✳ Larger tubs or washtubs: for placing under plants being potted, so as not to mess up the whole space.

Tips for re-potting

✳ Make sure all of your desired containers have sufficient drainage holes and create more if necessary (banging nails on to a block of wood held as a buffer inside the bucket helps).
✳ Get all of your plants out and give them a good soak with water prior to planting.
✳ Line very holey containers, such as baskets or rusty buckets, with plastic by stapling into place with a staple gun.
✳ Place large chips of broken pot over the holes in the base of the container to ensure the escape route for excess water is not blocked, but at the same time not too free-draining.

✳ Add a minimum 5cm (2in) layer of pebbles or gravel to the base to help anchor the plant and reduce your compost needs. Lightweight granules can be found for roof terraces or other areas where excess weight, particularly when the plants are wet, might be a problem.
✳ Sprinkle in a little soil mixed with compost around the base, along with a handful of slow-release fertilizer, such as blood, fish and bone.
✳ Plant the largest plants, such as trees or shrubs, first, digging a hole at least as large again as the original container and firming down new soil around the roots.
✳ Arrange all the other smaller plants – still in their nursery containers or, if dug up from the garden, in clumps of soil – on the soil around the larger plant. Adjust them according to height and colour, standing back to take stock on several occasions.
✳ When the desired effect has been achieved, gently knock the plants out of their pots, dig appropriately sized holes in your chosen positions and pop the plants in place, filling in around them with soil mixed with compost. Pat the soil down gently with your hands around the base of the stem of each plant and water well.
✳ Keep an eye on young plants in their first few weeks outside, particularly if the weather is dry. Give them a good soaking every few days (this is better for root development than watering every day).
✳ If, at any point, the roots of a plant protrude excessively through the holes in the base of the pot, that means the plant has outgrown the container and needs potting-on once. Simply repeat the process described above.
✳ For some ideas for recycled containers, see pages 84–9.

Patterns

The patterns we have used are very simple and, in most cases, consist of a hard outline with a dotted line if there is a seam allowance or a line of stitching. Follow the instructions for how many pieces to cut and where material needs to be doubled and/or placed on a fold. In some instances there are other markings that need to be transferred such as seam allowances and button and buttonhole positions.

Provided the pattern does not need sizing up, trace the outline plus any other detailing on to tracing paper. Pin the paper on to the fabric, as instructed, and cut around the fabric – also cutting through the paper, if this is the first time you have used the pattern. Using pinking shears can help prevent fraying on straight edges. Transfer any extra markings to the fabric using dressmaker's chalk – check that it comes out of the fabric easily. In the case of button positions or a seam allowance, you may prefer to place a pin in the correct place for reference, making sure the place where the pin disappears beneath the fabric to come up again is at the precise position that you want to record. You could also use a water-soluble pen or a tailor's tack. The latter is illustrated on the website http://sewing. about.com/library/sewnews/library/aamarking0404a.htm. By far the easiest way to scale up the patterns (such as the Child's summer dress on page 238) is to use a photocopier, enlarging by the percentage increase indicated on the pattern.

Egg cosies

See project on page 20
Enlarge pattern to 150% to get to actual size required

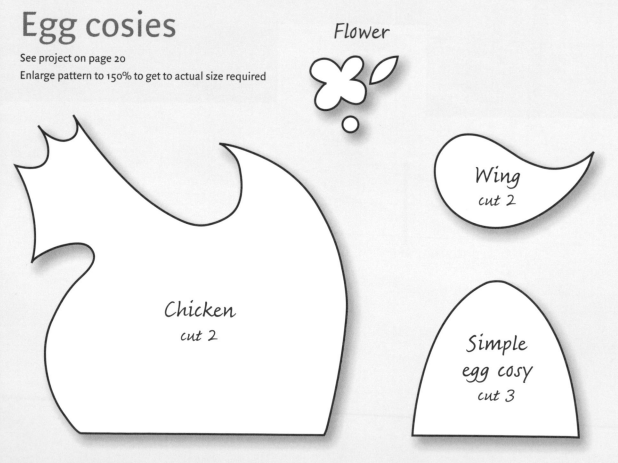

Flower

Chicken
cut 2

Wing
cut 2

Simple
egg cosy
cut 3

Lavender cats

See project on page 62
Enlarge pattern to 140% to get to
actual size required

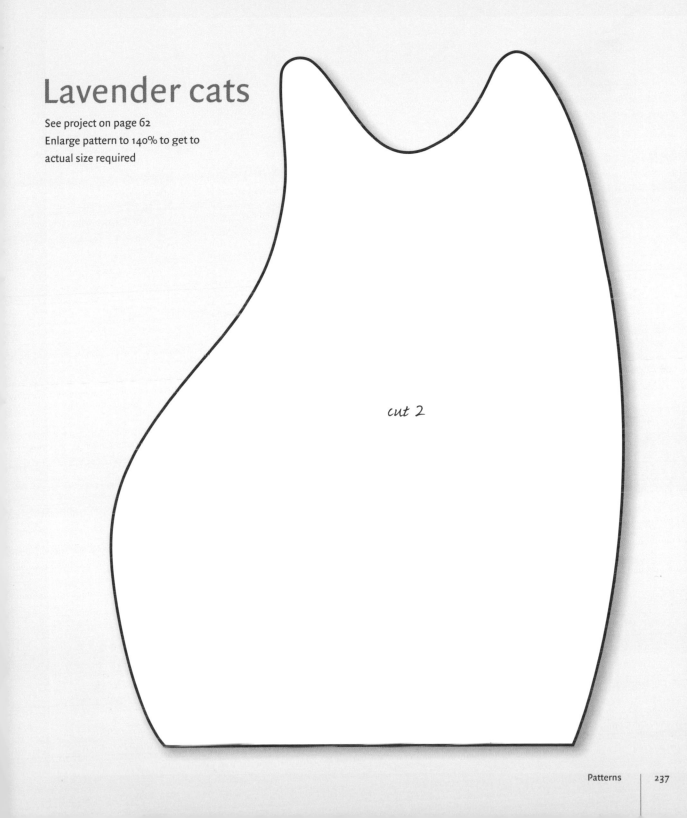

cut 2

Child's summer dress

See project on page 70
Enlarge pattern to 265% to get to
actual size required

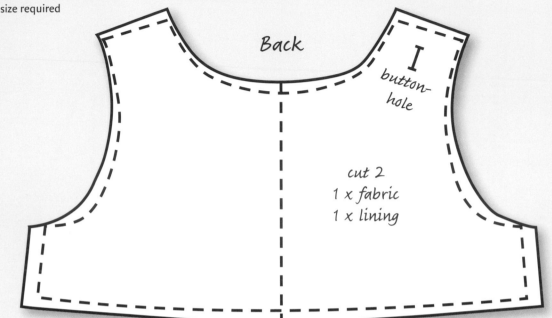

Back

I
button-
hole

cut 2
1 x fabric
1 x lining

Inner dotted line for age 1   Outer solid line for age 3

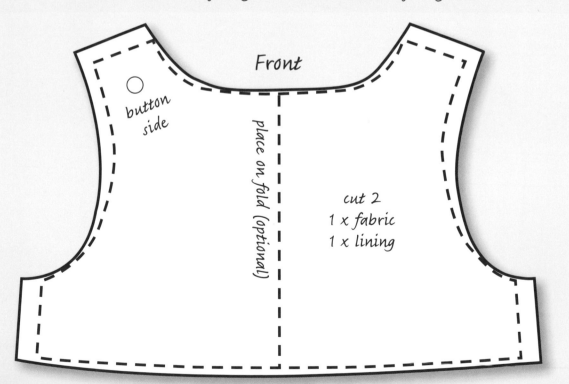

Front

○ button
side

place on fold (optional)

cut 2
1 x fabric
1 x lining

Skirt

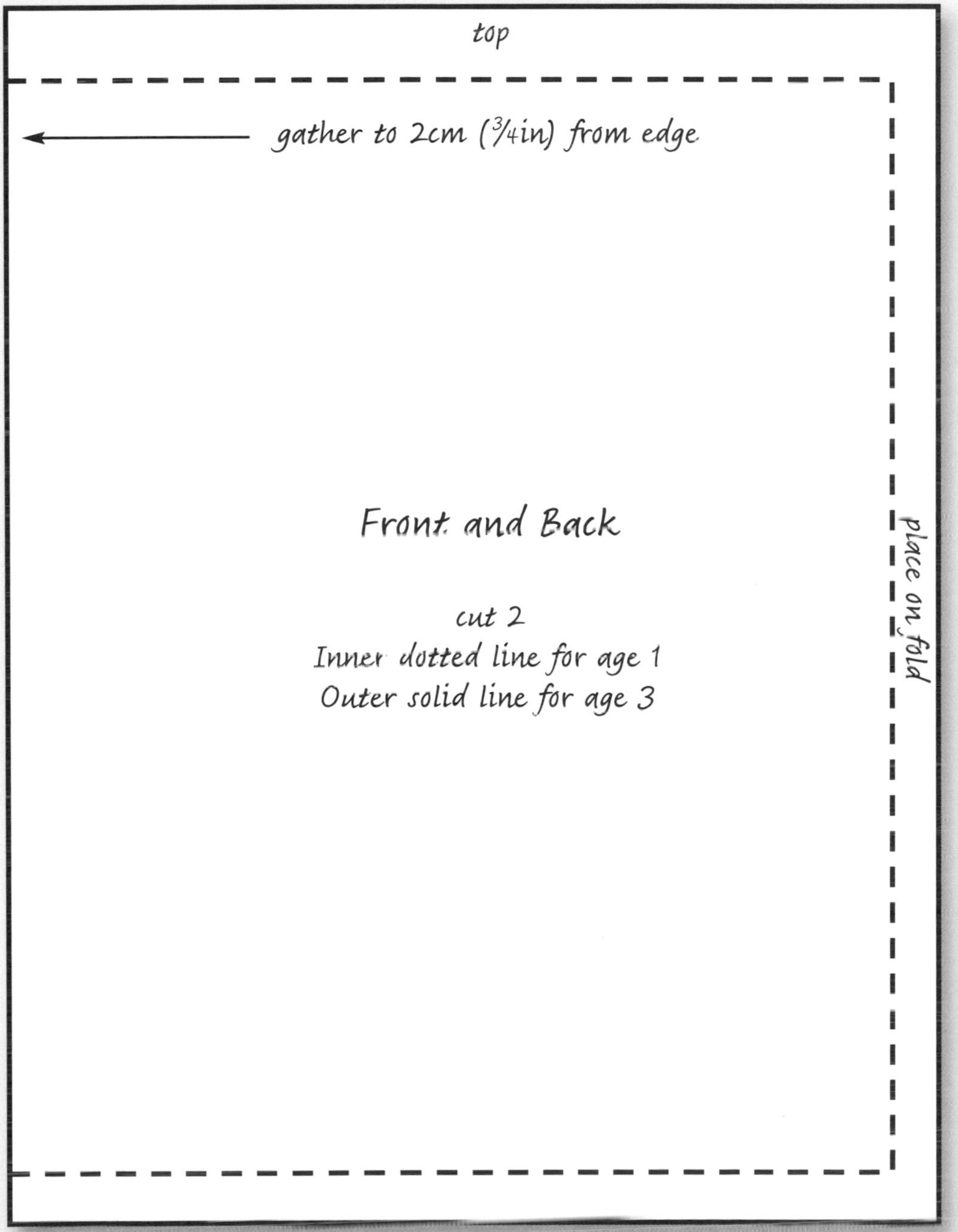

top

gather to 2cm (¾in) from edge ←

Front and Back

cut 2
Inner dotted line for age 1
Outer solid line for age 3

place on fold

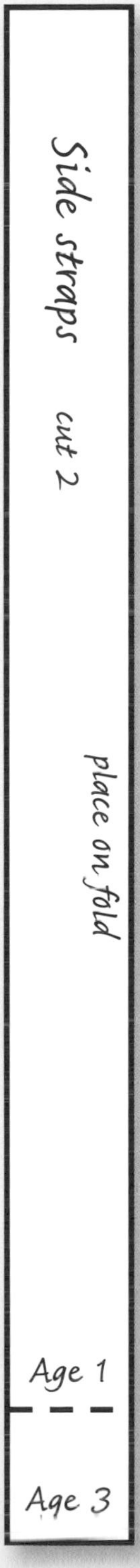

Side straps   cut 2

place on fold

Age 1

Age 3

Tea cosy and Beach bag

See projects on pages 138 (Tea cosy) and 100 (Beach bag)

Illustrations are drawn actual size

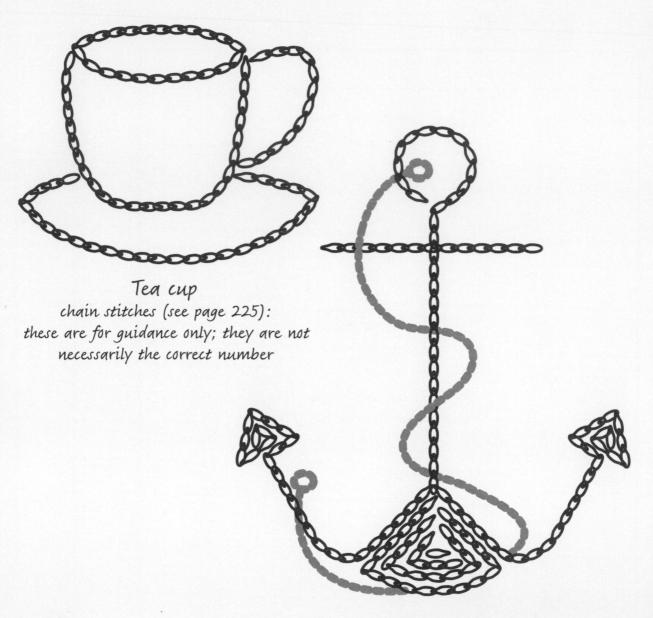

Tea cup
chain stitches (see page 225):
these are for guidance only; they are not
necessarily the correct number

Anchor
chain stitches (see page 225): these are for guidance
only; they are not necessarily the correct number.
Blue is rope ribbon wrapped around anchor

Christmas decorations

See project on page 216

Enlarge patterns to 143% to get to actual size required

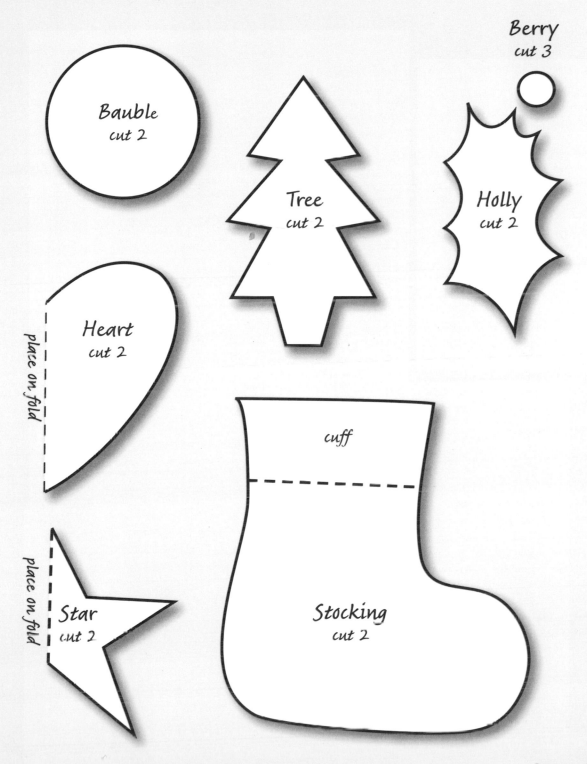

Bauble
cut 2

Tree
cut 2

Berry
cut 3

Holly
cut 2

Heart
cut 2

place on fold

cuff

Star
cut 2

place on fold

Stocking
cut 2

Directory

Decoration and inside projects

Shops and mail-order suppliers

earthBorn Paints
T 01928 734171 for stockists
www.earthbornpaints.co.uk
One of the highest eco-rated UK paint companies, has a new 'Pro Aqua' eggshell, which is oil and acrylic free and comes in some lovely sludgy greens, grey-blues and creams.

Farrow & Ball
T 01202 876141 for stockists
www.farrow-ball.com
Farrow & Ball do all their luscious colours in an Outdoor Eggshell and have just started doing a low VOC (low toxin) Estate Eggshell, which is great for inside if you are addicted to their colours but want to go a bit greener.

JustWipe
T 01606 836179
www.justwipe.co.uk
Large collection of oilcloths.

Oilcloth UK
www.oilcloth.co.uk
Wide choice of oilcloths, including colourful, gaudy Mexican designs.

Papers & Paints
T 020 7352 8626
www.papers-paints.co.uk
Check out their 'Historical' range for unusual shades that would suit both period and modern styles.

Paperchase
T 0161 839 1500
www.paperchase.co.uk
Great for general art and stationery supplies, including lots of different cards and papers (some beautiful handmade ones, at a price), paints and glue.

Russell and Chapple
68 Drury Lane, London WC2B 5SP
T 020 7836 7521
www.russellandchapple.co.uk
Old-fashioned but extremely efficient arts suppliers, selling everything from canvas and scrim-cloth to professional painting supplies. Online service also.

Shepherd's Bookbinders
76 Southampton Row, London WC1B 4AR
T 020 7831 1151
www.bookbinding.co.uk
One of the best sources of unusual papers for everything from bookbinding to card making – plus great online shop.

Websites

www.dmgantiquefairs.com: Lists up-and-coming prime antiques fairs.
www.salvo.co.uk: An international directory of UK suppliers of architectural salvage, from used timber, bricks, stone and cast iron to smaller items, such as garden furniture and pots.

Books

Contemporary Country by Ali Hanan and Emily Chalmers (Ryland, Peters & Small)
Inspiring book with gorgeous pictures showing made and bought goodies, both vintage and modern, combined to great effect.

Flea Market Style by Emily Chalmers (Ryland, Peters & Small)
Beautiful photos of stylish interiors focusing on vintage style and how to put together interiors using bric-a-brac and vintage finds. The book also has its own directory with tips and ideas of what to buy and where you might find bargains.

Junk Style by Melanie Molesworth (Ryland, Peters & Small)
Full of lots of good ideas, this book shows how to take one person's junk and turn it into a focus point in your home. It also illustrates how you can have confidence in your own style, taking things that others have no use for and recycling them into domestic treasure.

Sewing

Useful organizations

Northern Ireland Embroidery Guild
www.nieg.org.uk
No address given, but excellent
workshops in embroidery, felting and
beadwork.

Royal School of Needlework
Appartment 12A, Hampton Court Palace,
East Molesey, Surrey KT8 9AU
T 020 3166 6932
www.royal-needlework.co.uk
Charity whose mission is to teach, practise
and promote the art of hand embroidery
to the highest standards, within both
historical and contemporary design
contexts. Offers a variety of courses for
beginners to highly experienced
needleworkers, including one-day courses
or year-long training. Tours of their
inspiring collection of needlework through
the ages and of their studio are also
available – all in the genteel surroundings
of Hampton Court Palace.

Shops and mail-order suppliers

The Cloth House
47 Berwick Street, London W1F 8SJ
T 020 7437 5155
www.clothhouse.com
Vintage trimmings and ribbons alongside
the huge range of natural fabrics on offer.

The Cotton Patch
1285 Stratford Road, Hall Green,
Birmingham B28 9AJ
T 0121 702 2840

www.cottonpatch.co.uk
Fantastic shop and website specializing in
patchwork fabrics and accessories, books
and so on.

Duttons for Buttons
Oxford Street, Harrogate,
North Yorkshire HG1 1QE
T 01423 502092
www.duttonsforbuttons.co.uk
Fantastic shop bursting with all manner of
buttons and haberdashery. Supplies by
mail order. See website for other outlets.

Exeter Sewing Machine Company
7 Heavitree Road, Exeter,
Devon EX1 2LD
T 01392 275660
www.exetersewing.co.uk
Great source of thread, fabric and general
supplies for avid seamstresses.

In-Fabrics
12 Old Bridge, Haverfordwest,
Pembrokeshire SA61 2ET
T 01437 769164
www.in-fabrics.com
More than 2,000 rolls of fabric in stock!

Kleins
5 Noel Street, London W1F 8GD
T 020 7437 6162
www.kleins.co.uk
Chaos reins in this Soho institution, but
chances are they will have what you want
… plus they do mail order.

Lady Sew and Sew
Moy House, 57 Insitute Road,
Marlow, Buckinghamshire SL7 1BN
T 01628 890532

www.ladysewandsew.com
Fabric shop selling quilting, haberdashery
and sewing kits.

Liberty
Regent Street, London W1B 5AH
T 020 7734 1234
www.liberty.co.uk
This wonderful shop is an all-time classic
– its olde worlde appearance belies its up-
to-date and stylish stock – both the
haberdashery and furnishing
departments are brilliant, and walking
round the whole shop will provide plenty
of inspiration for projects of all kinds.

MacCulloch & Wallis
25–26 Dering Street, London W1S 1AT
T 020 7629 0311
www.macculloch-wallis.co.uk
Old-fashioned fabric shop selling all sorts
of dress trimmings and materials, as well
as good haberdashery supplies.

Mandors
131 East Claremont Street,
Edinburgh EH7 4JA
T 0131 558 3888
www.mandors.co.uk
Great supply of dressmaking and
furnishing materials.

Millers Creativity Shop
28 Stockwell St, Glasgow G1 4RT
T 0141 553 1660
www.millers-art.co.uk
Creative superstore with plenty of sewing
equipment.

Sew Creative
97–99 King Street, Cambridge CB1 1LD
T 01223 350691
www.sewcreative.co.uk
Suppliers of Pfaff and Singer sewing
machines along with a good range of
yarn and fabric.

The Sewing Bee
52 Hillfooot Street, Dunoon,
Argyll PA23 7DT
T 01369 706879
www.thesewingbee.co.uk
Gorgeous bijou haberdasher's shop.

Singer and Pfaff Sewing Centre
2 Queen Street, Penzance,
Cornwall TR18 4BJ
T 01736 363457
www.iriss.co.uk/Singer/index.htm
Supplier of sewing machines.

Samuel Taylor
10 Central Road, Leeds LS1 6DE
T 0113 245 9737
www.clickoncrafts.co.uk
Old-fashioned haberdasher that has a
great modern online shop.

VV Rouleaux
www.vvrouleaux.com
Famous ribbon specialists with fabulous
selection in many colours and widths.
See website for branches in London,
Newcastle and Glasgow.

Websites

www.betsyrosspatterns.com: Easy-to-
follow sewing patterns that can be
ordered online.
www.ciaspalette.com: Well-chosen
selection of quilting fabrics with a
personal touch from Cia herself.
www.clothkits.co.uk: The original
Seventies designs reworked for today in
those trademark 'cut out and snip to size'
patterns.
www.equilter.com: Fabrics for sale, plus
'design board' feature that allows you to
try them out in thumbnail samples.
www.fitzpatterns.com: Fashionably funky
patterns to download for girls and boys –
many of them free.
www.gloriouscolor.com: American
quilter's site, but will ship fabrics to the
UK.
www.jkneedles.com: Materials and
accessories for all kinds of needlework,
including beginners' kits and videos and
DVDs.
www.opheliabutton.co.uk: Jewellery and
other treasures made from beautiful
vintage buttons.
www.sewessential.co.uk: Range of
haberdashery and sewing supplies.
www.sewing.org: Instructions on a wide
range of techniques, including fashion
sewing and creating pet clothes, making
a skirt from a pair of jeans and other
contemporary styles.
www.sewmamasew.com: Fab fabrics in
all styles.
www.vpll.org: Fascinating pattern library
featuring designs from 1840 to 1950 with
vintage publications too.

Books

Colourful Stitchery by Kristin Nicholas
(Storey Books)
Wonderful exuberant embroidery to
inspire and delight.

The Gentle Art of Domesticity by
Jane Brocket (Hodder & Stoughton)
Jane Brocket's wonderful website,
www.yarnstorm.co.uk (see page 251),
really put sewing, knitting and patchwork
back on the map.

The Quilts of Gee's Bend by John Beardsley
(Atlanta)
Fascinating, moving account of the
history and women behind these
amazing, irregular quilts that break all
the rules and yet are inspiring and
beautiful.

*Mary Thomas's Dictionary of Embroidery
Stitches* by Mary Thomas (Caxton Editions)
A real classic, as recommended by author
Jane Brocket (see above), founder of
Yarnstorm (see website on page 251).

Knitting and crochet

Useful organizations

Knitting and Crochet Guild
www.knitting-and-crochet-guild.org.uk/
An amazing organization set-up to
promote and encourage the crafts of
hand knitting, machine knitting and
crochet. Aimed at makers that are also
interested in the history of knitting and
crochet, it is full of information and links
to archival material to do with the yarn
arts. It runs classes too. See the website
for local contacts.

UK Hand Knitting Association
www.ukhandknitting.com
A mine of information on classes, knitting
groups, shows and shops.

Victoria and Albert Museum
Cromwell Road, London SW7 2RL
T 020 7942 2000
www.vam.ac.uk
Has a great website – type 'knitting' into
the seach box for everything from the
history of knitting to the best shops, free
patterns and blogs.

Knitting and crochet classes

Learning from other people is the best
way to start any new craft – either one-on-
one with a friend or relative or in a group
of friends or local people interested in
extending their skills. There are also
various 'knitting gurus' offering tailor-
made classes for individuals or groups.

Ros Badger, co-author of this book, offers
knitting lessons at her home in South
London (www.rosbadger.com) as well as
groups for children, and her book *Instant
Expert: Knitting* is full of inspirational
photographs and is the first stop for
anyone wanting to learn knitting.

Shops and mail-order suppliers

Loop
41 Cross Stitch, London N1 2BB
T 020 7288 1160
www.loop.gb.com
Fine-looking shop stuffed to the gunwales
with lovely candy-coloured yarns. You can
also drop in for emergency knitting advice
or enrol in lunchtime classes. Online
shopping available.

Stash Yarns
213 Upper Richmond Road,
London SW15 6SQ
T 020 8246 6666
www.stashyarns.co.uk
Another great shop selling yarns from
around the world – with a good online
ordering service, too.

Web of Wool
53 Regent Grove, Holly Walk,
Leamington Spa,
Warwickshire CV32 4PA
T 01926 311614
www.webofwool.co.uk
Specializes in self-patterning wools that
knit or crochet up in different colours
without the need to change wools. A great
source of knitting and crochet yarn and
supplies, the shop is cheerful, inspiring
and well stocked, and the online ordering
service efficient.

Websites

www.angelyarns.com
www.castoff.info: Radical knitting
website – featuring a hysterical knitted
wedding.
www.colinette.com: An unusual range of
hand-dyed yarns in many different colour
combinations that you won't find
elsewhere.
www.coolwoolz.co.uk/shop/index.php
www.cornishorganicwool.co.uk
www.cucumberpatch.co.uk
www.dominknitrix.com: For no-
nonsense, straight-talking help on
knocking your knitting into shape – as
funny as it is informative.
www.ecoknits.co.uk
www.farmyarn.co.uk
www.kangaroo.uk.com
www.knitty.com: An amazing US-based
resource for knitters, offering free
patterns, articles and technical advice for
novices and experienced knitters alike –
all spooled out with welcome warmth and
humour in an online periodical magazine
format.
www.laughinghens.com: Online wool
store with a good range of patterns,
yarns, kits, accessories and books.
www.louet.com: For finest quality
Euroflax linen in an inspiring range of
colours.
www.shetland-wool-brokers.zetnet.co.uk
www.mazzmatazz.co.uk: Site of the
original 'rebel knitter' who designed
cuddly versions of Dr Who villains along
with other weird and wonderful stuff.
www.nextstitch.com: Easy-to-read
crochet patterns for ponchos, shawls
and other accessories – even bikinis.

www.ravelry.com: Like Facebook for knitters – you can share projects, tips and chat with like-minded fellow-knitters.
www.simplysockyarn: American company with a great list of yarns from all the top producers.
www.stitchnbitch.co.uk: For local group knitting and general craft-club gossip while you knit, or look at your local press and craft/art shop windows.
www.texere.co.uk: All kinds of yarn, plus chenille, metallic yarns and embroidery thread.
www.theknittinghut.com
www.ysolda.com: Website of lovely young Scottish knitter.

Books

Complete Guide to Knitting and Crochet by Nicki French (Parragon)
Great illustrations and an informative, easy-to-follow style of writing. The book includes plenty of simple but interesting projects that even beginners can master.

The Crochet Answer Book: Solutions to Every Problem You'll Ever Face by Edie Eckman (Storey)
A useful addition to your crochet library.

Essential Crochet: 30 Irresistible Projects for You and Your Home by Erika Knight (Quadrille)
A lovely book full of stylish up-to-date crochet projects for the home.

The Harmony Guides: Crochet Stitch Motifs: 250 to Crochet and Basic Crochet Stitches: 250 to Crochet (Harmony Guides series, Interweave Press) edited by Erika Knight

Two great books full of crochet stitches and edited by excellent knitting and crochet guru Erika Knight.

Knit and Purl Stitches by Erica Knight
Colour photos instruct on the basic and not-so-basic stitches necessary for a real knitter. Good for beginners, and also those wanting to graduate beyond the novice stocking and garter stitches.

Knitty Gritty by Aneeta Patel (A&C Black)
Full of beginner-proof instructions and patterns.

Kyuuto! Japanese Crafts: Lacy Crochet and Kyuuto! Japanese Crafts (Chronicle Books)
Quirky patterns with a Japanese view on crochet.

Loop Vintage Crochet by Susan Cropper (Jacqui Small)
A beautifully presented and inspiring book by the owner of the Loop shop in London (see page 245).

Mason-Dixon Knitting: The Curious Knitter's Guide and Mason-Dixon Knitting: Outside the Lines by Kay Gardiner and Ann Meador Shayne (Crown Publications)
Stories, patterns, advice, opinions, questions, answers, jokes and pictures from two American knitting friends.

Stitch 'n' Bitch Handbook: Instructions, Patterns and Advice for a New Generation of Knitters by Debbie Stoller (Workman Publishing)
The book that kick-started the recent knitting revolution and still very useful as well as surprising and entertaining.

Gardening and outdoor projects

Useful organizations

Garden Organic
Ryton Organic Gardens, near Coventry, Warwickshire CV8 3LG
T 02476 303517
www.gardenorganic.org.uk
Formerly known as the Henry Doubleday Research Association, this is the gardening arm of the Soil Association and is geared to smaller-scale gardeners, especially those growing their own organic food. Its show gardens demonstrating the latest organic growing methods are a must to visit (free to members) while the Heritage Seed Library offers members a chance to grow and help protect rare heirloom varieties of fruits and vegetables.

National Society of Allotment and Leisure Gardeners
T 01536 266576
www.nsalg.org.uk
Champions of UK allotment sites and the place to contact for information about allotment sites in your area.

Royal Horticultural Society (RHS)
80 Vincent Square, London SW1P 2PE
T 020 7834 4333
www.rhs.org.uk
Britain's largest gardening charity, renowned for its outstanding gardens, inspirational flower shows, research and educational programmes. Membership is a rite of passage for those whose curiosity about gardening has extended beyond the local garden centre, and includes free

entry to the RHS gardens and London shows, a monthly issue of the excellent *The Garden* magazine and privileged entry on specified days to the national RHS flower shows, including Chelsea, Hampton Court and Tatton Park.

Nurseries and mail-order suppliers

Bulbs

Avon Bulbs
T 01460 242177
www.avonbulbs.co.uk
Visitors to the Chelsea Flower Show will be familiar with this company's beautiful display stands, packed with all manner of exquisite small bulbs, some of them rare.

Bloms Bulbs
T 01234 709099
www.blomsbulbs.com
For paperwhites (see page 192), prepared hyacinths and a wide variety of tulips, alliums, lilies and other bulbs, sold in small batches.

Peter Nyssen
T 0161 747 4000
www.peternyssen.com
For larger quantities of bulbs (50 or more – for doing batches of paperwhites or hyacinths as presents (see page 192)), this wholesale supplier offers a no-frills catalogue but great bulbs competitively priced.

Seeds and plants

Beth Chatto Gardens and Nursery
Elmstead Market,
Colchester, Essex CO7 7DB
T 01206 822007
www.bethchatto.co.uk
Nursery and inspirational gardens created by the UK's greatest living plantswoman. The gardens are divided into dry, wet and woodland areas, with corresponding sections of plants in the nursery (also mail order), so all growing conditions are catered for.

John Chambers Wildflower Seeds
T 01933 652562
www.johnchamberswildflowerseeds.co.uk
For wildflower and grass seed, including many mixes for specific areas and even a 'wildflower windowbox' mixture.

Fentongollan Vegetable Plants by Post
T 01872 520209
www.flowerfarm.co.uk/Vegetables-by-Post/
Reasonably priced plants raised in Cornwall for commercial growers and packed in 'mini greenhouses' so they can happily wait a week or more before planting out. For herb and vegetable seedlings for an 'instant' vegetable garden: dig the patch or find the containers one weekend and plant up the next.

Ken Muir
Honeypot Farm, Rectory Road,
Weeley Heath, Clacton-on-Sea,
Essex CO16 9BJ
T 01255 83018
www.kenmuir.co.uk

Great fruit nursery run by one of the country's real specialists. Excellent for strawberry plants, small fruit trees and soft fruit canes and bushes.

Organic Gardening Catalogue
T 0845 1301304
www.organiccatalogue.com
The mail-order arm of the excellent organic gardening association Garden Organic (see left), stocking a high percentage of organic seed and seed potatoes, plus useful gardening equipment from water butts to raised beds and mini polytunnels for raising salad leaves in winter.

Petersham Nurseries
off Petersham Road, Petersham,
Richmond TW10 7AG
T 020 8940 5230
www.petershamnurseries.com
No mail order, but a great selection of plants, seeds, gardening supplies and gifts in the most stylish of settings. The ever-more-fashionable café, with delicious food, much of it cooked from produce grown on site, is well worth visiting – book first for lunch.

Plant World
St Marychurch Road, Newton Abbot,
Devon TQ12 4SE
T 01803 872939
www.plant-world-seeds.com
A plantsman's nursery with a garden planted to represent the five continents, each area spilling over with exotic plants from the appropriate region. The catalogue is full of flowering treats, the seed always fresh and properly packaged.

Sarah Raven's Cutting Garden
T 01672 871715
www.sarahraven.com
Possibly not the cheapest source of seed
or young flower and kitchen garden
seedlings, but the varieties have been
picked by Sarah Raven, whose florist's
eye for flowers and passion for trialling
vegetables at her Sussex garden (open at
various times during the year) mean
you're guaranteed a good show.

Seeds of Italy
T 020 8427 5020
www.seedsofitaly.com
A great catalogue for people wishing to
combine a love of gardening with a taste
for Mediterranean cooking. Seeds for the
ingredients of all your favourite dishes –
including many varieties of basil, borlotti
beans and crinkly dark green cavolo nero
– are offered in their attractive and very
generous Franchi packaging.

Simpson's Seeds
The Walled Garden Nursery,
Horningsham, Warminster,
Wiltshire BA12 7NQ
T 01985 845004
www.simpsonsseeds.co.uk
A family run business specializing in
seeds (and young plants) of unusual
tomato and pepper varieties, including
some red-hot exotic chillis. The nursery
and walled garden are open to the public,
and a wider variety of young plants is sold
on site.

Special Plants
Greenway Lane, Cold Ashton,
Chippenham, Wiltshire SN14 8LA
T 01225 891686
www.specialplants.net
A wonderful nursery selling seeds of many
rare and beautiful garden plants by mail
order and on site to visitors. There are
also some great courses run by nursery
owner Derry Watkins.

Suffolk Herbs
Monks Farm, Coggeshall Road,
Kelvedon, Essex CO5 9PG
T 01376 572456
www.suffolkherbs.com
Another great source for organic
gardeners, with seed for herbs,
wildflowers and unusual vegetable
varieties – the catalogue even offers
alternative health products, dried herbs
and spices and organic wines alongside.

Wiggly Wigglers
T 01981 500391
www.wigglywigglers.co.uk
Their excellent catalogue (more of a
source book for organic gardeners)
includes composting supplies and birdfood ranges (see opposite) as well as a
new range of 'ready-to-plant vegetable
plots', consisting of various collections of
salad and vegetable seedlings.

Woottens of Wenhaston
Halesworth, Suffolk IP19 9HD
T 01502 478258
www.woottensplants.co.uk
One of the best nurseries in the country,
with an inspirational show garden that
looks good from spring to late summer.
Great selection of plants that are sent out

beautifully packed in biodegradable
packaging. Also some impressive seasonal
offers if you get on their mailing list.

Other gardening supplies

Green Gardener
T 01603 715096
www.greengardener.co.uk
For all manner of ecological gardening
supplies, with natural pest control for
everything from slugs and snails to green,
black and whitefly a speciality. Their
advice line is excellent.

Harrod Horticultural
T 0845 402 5300
www.harrodhorticultural.com
Good general-purpose mail-order
suppliers of everything from tools and
propagators to DIY raised wooden beds
and fruit cages for kitchen gardens.

Organic Gardening Catalogue
See page 247.

Plantstuff
T 0870 7743366
www.plantstuff.com
One of the most stylish garden
accessories suppliers around, with
beautiful pots, tools and general
gardening gear.

Wiggly Wigglers
See left.

Birds

CJ Wildlife
T 0800 731 2820
www.birdfood.co.uk
A wide range of feeders, nest boxes and various types of birdfood.

Wiggly Wigglers
See left.
Also included in their excellent general catalogue, the separate Bird Deli brochure packed with all sorts of bird feeding equipment and food mixes, including live worms.

Books

The Organic Garden: Green Gardening for a Healthy Planet by Allan Shepherd (Collins)
Written with great honesty and humour as well as authoritative first-hand experience.

The RHS Plant Finder (Dorling Kindersley)
Must-have directory updated annually that tells you which nursery or supplier has exactly the plant you are after.

Cooking and kitchen projects

Useful organizations

Slow Food
www.slowfood.com
Starting in Italy, the influence of the excellent Slow Food Movement – championing the homemade over the mass-produced, the local and seasonal above the shipped-in from overseas, and now often known as just the Slow Movement – has spread to other areas, including gardening, travel and, increasingly, home-making.

Shops and mail-order suppliers

Jane Asher Party Cakes and Sugarcraft
T 020 7584 6177
www.jane-asher.co.uk
A huge range of good-quality equipment and supplies for making and decorating cakes.

Divertimenti
www.divertimenti.co.uk
Shops and mail order with wide range of pots, pans, knives and all things made for the kitchen.

Ecko Bakeware
Available from www.Pots-and-Pans.co.uk
(T 01877 339900) or Paton Calvert at www.paton-calvert.co.uk
(T 02380 780555).

Lakeland Ltd
T 01539 488100
www.lakelandlimited.com

Great for general cooking ware, and all the items – jam pans, funnels, jars, bottles, labels and so on – necessary for the jam-making and tipple-brewing projects.

John Lewis
T 08456 049 049 for nearest outlet
www.johnlewis.com
Amazing source of all things to do with cooking and baking and home-making generally. Just walking around one of their stores makes one feel inspired and full of virtuous intentions.

Squires
T 0845 2255671
www.squires-shop.com
The website is devoted to kitchen aids and baking ware – a great source of cutters and icing equipment.

Summerill and Bishop
100 Portland Road, London W11 4LN
T 020 7221 4566
www.summerillandbishop.com
Designer cookware from all around the world.

Books

Cafe Paradiso Seasons by Dennis Cotter (Hylas Publishing)
A proper cookbook for vegetarians. No lentil bakes and homity pie here, just lovely creative recipes using seasonal food and combining wonderful flavours in the Pacific Rim style of Skye Gyngell (see overleaf) but without the meat.

Cupcakes Magic: Little Cakes with Attitude by
Kate Shirazi (Pavilion)
Has some wonderfully creative – and
occasionally eccentric – ideas for
cupcakes.

Delia Smith Complete Cookery Course by
Delia Smith (BBC Books)
You still can't beat Delia for down-to-
earth, easy-to-follow advice on cooking
everything from the perfect sponge to
roast potatoes that are crunchy every
time.

Falling Cloudberries by Tessa Kiros
(Murdoch Books)
A cookbook with heart, weaving Kiros's
own family heritage with mouthwatering
recipes, many handed down through
generations.

New Cranks by Nadine Abensur (Orion)
A vegetarian cookbook that inspires and
is as far from the wholemeal everything
approach of old Cranks as possible –
great combinations of ingredients and
particularly good for tart recipes.

A Year in my Kitchen and *Favourite
Ingredients* by Skye Gyngell (Quadrille)
Books that are as beautiful as they are
practical by the chef at the ever-inspiring
Petersham Nursery Café. Seasonal food
created with a fresh and different
approach, using a 'toolbox' of flavourings
to give depth and richness to the recipes.

General sites and suppliers we like

Some of these are places where we buy
items we love, others (the more expensive
among them) are where we go to get
inspired. Exposing yourself to as much
good-quality and beautiful material,
whether it is clothes or furniture or food,
is great for getting the mind going and
thinking of your own ideas to create.
It's not plagiarism – slavish copying is
definitely not on the agenda – it's more
letting one person's ideas and creativity
inspire your own.

Mary Mathieson: An artist with a special
interest in working with flowers, who did
some of the illustrations and made many
of the projects in this book. She can be
contacted on 07940 919622.

www.baileyshomeandgarden.com:
Classic, stylish products for the house and
garden, many recycled and with an
original twist. Their huge showroom shop
in Wales is worth a visit.

www.caravanstyle.com: Stylist Emily
Chalmers set up this gorgeous shop
specializing in vintage thrift in the most
stylish way possible.

www.charlenemullen.com: Incredibly
talented textile designer specializing in
cushions and homeware – rather
expensive, but handmade using the most
sumptuous fabrics and a real inspiration.

www.coxandcox.co.uk: Pretty and useful
accessories for the home, but particularly
good on bits and pieces for making
things, from lovely snowflake cookie
cutters to letter printing and stamping
sets.

www.designspongeonline.com: Lovely
things noticed and described with an
observant and original eye.

www.frankworks.eu: Based in Whitstable
on the north Kent coast, this is a place for
British alternative applied arts and
contemporary craft – books and badges,
jewellery and stationery, textiles, prints,
ceramics and lighting that are often
handmade, original, quirky or downright
eccentric.

www.fredbare.co.uk: For some of the
most stylish hats in town. The lovely shop
at 118 Columbia Road, London E2 7RG
(01904 624579) is usually only open on
Sundays so ring or email via the website
for more details.

www.helpyourshelf.co.uk: Lovely website
and shop full of unique and stylish
objects.

www.indiangardencompany.co.uk:
Suppliers of beautiful garden accessories
including the lovely umbrella used on
page 108.

www.kitchengarden-hens.co.uk: Francine Raymond's site, based at her Suffolk cottage, where hens run free in the garden and often stray into the house and yard where Francine runs her small but perfectly formed (and very reasonably priced) hen and garden accessories business. Items on sale in her Christmas shop inspired the Artichoke candle-holders on page 130.

www.labourandwait.co.uk: Timeless, functional products for the house and garden.

www.liiviantalossa.blogspot.com: You don't need to speak Finnish to appreciate this photographer's blog with its sensitive, beautiful photographs (oh, that Nordic light) documenting the homely (and naturally stylish) domestic life of Liivian and her young daughter. Her fellow-Scandinavian's blog, Vintage Living at www.myblogvintageliving. blogspot.com is similarly inspiring.

www.papastour.com: Scottish arts and crafts with lots of lovely things plus a hideaway to rent.

www.pedlars.co.uk: Great, fun, original items, including many that aid creativity – kitchen kit (including fab 'Keep Calm and Carry ON' apron), old printers' blocks, vintage tins and reclaimed plant pots, old-fashioned cleaning equipment, sticky tape dispensers and so on.

www.plantsuff.co.uk: Great items for the garden, including lovely containers to plant up in style.

www.re-foundobjects.co.uk: 'Re' stands for 'recycled, restored, reused' – and the website (and fabulous shop in Northumberland – well worth stopping off on your way up to Scotland) is bristling with original finds and new ways to use old objects and fabrics, which can't help but be inspiring.

www.squintlimited.com: For heavenly (if pricey) original items, such as the patchwork sofa mentioned on page 64. Great for inspiring your own homespun versions.

www.tattersall-love.com/kristinperers/index.htm: The website for Kristen Perers' agent. Kristen is a talented stylist whose work inspired the patchwork throw on page 66.

www.yarnstorm.co.uk: The creation of the fantastically inspiring and prolific Jane Brocket, who knits, patchworks, cooks and gardens and posts her creations regularly online, this is one of the first and best of the many crafts websites, including knitting, sewing, embroidery and patchwork as well as cake baking.

Index

Acknowledgements

Firstly we would both like to thank Benjamin J Murphy for his perfectionist's eye and dedication - his photographs have made this book truly beautiful. Also Mary Mathieson for her wonderful illustrations, and for contributing so much to various projects throughout the book.

Huge thanks are also due to Jane Turnbull, our brilliant agent, who championed this idea from the start; Denise Bates and all at HarperCollins who took it up and ran with it and really went the extra measure to produce such a beautiful book; Andrew Barron for the elegant design; Emma Callery for her skilful editing and Charlotte Allen for all her hard work on publicity. We would also like to thank Piers Feltham and Chiara Menage, Christopher Matthews and Phillipa George and Caddy and Chris Wilmot-Sitwell for allowing us to take photographs in their gardens.

Many other people have helped inspire our own creativity and have contributed to this book in so many different ways. They include Vanessa Aitchison, Michael Badger, Jane Brocket, Carolyn Brookes-Davies, Karen Jensen-Jones, Carol Lloyd Waters, Karen Long, Gary Kaye, Monica McMillan, Lawrence Morton, Charlene Mullen, Kristin Perers, Francine Raymond, Maureen and Phil Rooksby, Jo Self and not forgetting craft club members especially Lorraine Sorrel, Caddy Wilmot-Sitwell, Kim West, Rebecca Tanqueray and Tessa Brown and 'knitting ladies' Katy Jaffey, Grace Hodge, Vicky Cryer and Sarah Bratby.
Thank you all!

Ros: I would also like to thank my mum Ruth Badger for teaching me to sew when I was very young, and her sister Joan Kenwright who, along with my mum, spent hours 'on the sewing machine' throughout my childhood; also my grandmother Mary Elizabeth Hunter for teaching me how to crochet when I was seven years old.

Elspeth: I would also like to thank my mother and father, Margaret and Alec Thompson for bringing me up in a home where making things was second nature, and my sisters Rebecca Edwards and Sarah Hanshaw, whose homes are filled with beautiful things they have made over many years. Thank you for all you have taught me – and the inspiration and encouragement.